Larder Lads

Just for the boys,
a collection of
mouthwatering,
simple recipes

**LOUISE HOLLAND &
ROBERTA MOORE**

EBURY PRESS
LONDON

Dedications

Roberta: To the men in my life who I couldn't do without – Matt, Freddie and Dean; to the new girl in my life, Ava Elizabeth, and to my mother, who is always there.

In memory of my late father, Bobby, who I miss every day.

Louise: For my parents, who have been supportive and attentive throughout my career. To my dear friend and partner, Steve. Also to my mate, Charlie, for keeping me on my toes!

In memory of my late brother John Kent, my friend of yesterday, today and forever, whose endless enthusiasm for my cooking in my early years was insurmountable.

Acknowledgements: Our thanks go to everyone who has helped us with this book, whatever form their help has taken. We've been lucky to have a very supportive circle of family and friends whose enthusiasm has almost matched our own. Special thanks to Amy, John and Tina for their support over the past year, and all the years before that. They've listened patiently to our suggestions, offered their advice regarding our concerns and provided us with ongoing encouragement. Our sincerest thanks to the following:

Everyone who came with title suggestions – you kept us laughing. Sorry if they're not included but most of them were a little too risqué. To Maz, who was there at the beginning, whose title this is and Andrew Conrad, who gave us a hilarious afternoon of help and advice on our writing skills. Also Diane Macfarlane and Mandie Turner, for their reading skills.

All at Ebury Press; in particular, Fiona MacIntyre for having faith in us and our idea.

Michael Caine, Jay Kay, Lennox Lewis, Johnny Herbert, Chris Evans, Johnny Vaughan, Teddy Sheringham and Pete Tong for their co-operation in providing their delicious recipes for the men of Britain to share.

And to Matt, whose vision and help have driven us forward. We really can't thank you enough.

First published in the United Kingdom in 2000 by Ebury Press
Random House
20 Vauxhall Bridge Road · London SW1V 2SA

Random House Australia (Pty) Limited
20 Alfred Street · Milsons Point · Sydney · New South Wales 2061 · Australia

Random House New Zealand Limited
18 Poland Road · Glenfield · Auckland 10 · New Zealand

Random House South Africa (Pty) Limited
Endulini · 5a Jubilee Road · Parktown 2193 · South Africa

Random House Group Limited Reg. No. 954009

A CIP catalogue record for this book is available from the British Library

ISBN: 0 09 187081 X

Designed by Lovelock & Co.
Photographs by Jason Moore
Edited by Jane Donovan

Printed and bound by Butler & Tanner Ltd, Frome and London

CONTENTS

FOREWORD

'How do you fancy cooking for Ronaldo on live television?' asked Louise, my old school friend.

To be honest, I didn't fancy it much. But with Louise's mantra of 'You'll be alright,' ringing in my ears I appeared on Channel Four's *Light Lunch* where she was the food consultant. Ronaldo, sadly, missed his flight, so with a late, but great, double substitution I made lunch for two footballers. In the bar after the show, I was complimented on my cooking.

'That was a winner,' remarked one of the England superstars.

'Thank you. Erm, do you cook much?'

'I'd like to have a go but it's all too complicated and I never seem to have the time.'

Then, like a Ronaldo thunderbolt, the idea for *Larder Lads* hit me. A man-friendly cookery book. Louise agreed it was worth a shot and the footballer thought so too, particularly when I pointed out the real way to a woman's heart was through the kitchen.

So if you spot a certain English football star in the aisles of his local supermarket rather than in a night club or on a golf course, you'll know he's bought our book. For his £14.99 and the inspiration, I thank him.

For Louise's cooking genius, I thank her.

Roberta Moore

INTRODUCTION

So there was *Light Lunch*, the footballer and now we had to write the book. But before we could start we had to establish exactly what a kitchen-phobic man needed and wanted from a cookery book.

There was only one place (well, actually two) to find them – our little black books. Once we had blown off the cobwebs we called our old flames still guaranteed to be single. We hunted and gathered all brands of men – young, single, divorced. Not wanting to leave out the marrieds, we also spoke to men who wanted to cook for their women.

Hours were spent on the phone, over lunch and over dinner. Needless to say, our female instincts were confirmed: men wanted foolproof, easy-to-follow recipes and that's what we have included here. Let's hope the suggestions turn you on to your kitchen and your women on to you!

Louise Holland

Note

Cooking temperatures and times for the recipes in this book are for fan ovens. If you are using a conventional oven, increase the heat by 10°C/50°F. Alternatively, for recipes with long cooking times, cook the dish at the temperature given for an additional 10 minutes per hour.

chapter one

handling your tools

Here's our What Not To Miss List. Each piece of equipment is discussed later on in this chapter.

Basic Utensils
- Knives: small paring knife, bread/carving knife, medium-sized knife, knife sharpener/steel
- Food processor (fittings are automatically purchased with it)
- Hand blender
- Electric whisk (with three settings)
- Frying pans
- Casseroles/saucepans
- Coffee grinder
- Pestle and mortar
- Roasting tins and baking trays
- Carbon steel wok
- Wooden or plastic chopping board
- Slotted wooden spoon
- Selection of wooden, metal and wire spoons (spiders)
- Small and medium ladles
- Glass Pyrex mixing bowls
- Tin opener
- Corkscrew
- Measuring scales
- Masher/ricer
- Flexible metal fish slice or turner
- Selection of spatulas
- Serrated palette knife
- Garlic crusher
- Hand (balloon) whisk
- Kitchen tongs
- Bowl scraper with rubber plastic handle
- Grater
- Zester
- Wooden pepper mill
- Colander and sieves
- Salad spinner
- Measuring jug
- Pastry brush
- Ice cream scoop
- Measuring spoons
- Kitchen timer
- Small plastic mandolin
- Potato peeler

Most men wouldn't consider playing their favourite sport without the right equipment. Imagine tackling a round at Gleneagles with a second-rate set of dilapidated golf clubs or playing football with a deflated beach ball. Yet lots of people still try and get away with using poor-quality kitchen equipment for their cooking.

Using the right basic equipment for cooking is very important and it really does make all the difference in making your life in the kitchen easier and the subsequent results more impressive. Some kitchen equipment is expensive, but seeing as it's something you'll be using almost every day, isn't it worth it?

Although we don't expect you to go out and equip your kitchen to the standard of a restaurant, it'll probably be helpful to have an idea of what you'll need to find your way around the recipes in this book. As the recipes cover all eventualities for a man of your stature, if you can collate the following equipment over a course of time, you'll be pretty much set up for life.

SAUCEPANS AND CASSEROLES

Where do you start on one of the biggest investments in your 'batterie de cuisine'? There are so many different varieties of saucepan available to the consumer these days, it's easy to become confused. Hopefully, we'll help make the decision-making process easier for you. Our list below outlines the types of saucepans that we consider best for all-round cooking and gives the sizes you should aim to have in your collection of kitchen equipment. An important point to remember when purchasing saucepans is to ensure that they feel good and strong. You don't want anything overly heavy or too light and flimsy.

Copper Saucepans These are the very best saucepans you can buy. Unfortunately, they are also very expensive but well worth it as they are a good, even conductor of heat and cool rapidly when taken off the heat. If you do choose to buy a set, make sure they are lined with stainless steel to make maintenance and cleaning easier.

Enamelled Cast-Ironware Very heavy, expensive and available in attractive bright colours, cast-ironware is a good conductor of heat. It doesn't handle well as a saucepan, but is excellent for roasting trays and lidded casseroles when a constant high or low heat is needed. Generally, it is not recommended to put this type of cookware in the dishwasher, so be prepared to wash up by hand.

Stainless Steel After copper, stainless steel is the best conductor of heat as nowadays these saucepans have heavy bases made out of layers of steel, copper and aluminium, which is important as a conductor of heat. They should have a good, strong metal handle. Although the handle may get hot, this means that you can start cooking on the hob and finish off in the oven. After you have burnt yourself once, you won't do it again! They are easy to clean and generally dishwasher safe.

Anodised There are many different types of anodised pans. These are aluminium pans which have been chemically treated. Doing this produces a much harder material. They are a very good conductor of heat and also provide a good-quality, non-stick surface. This type of finish is particularly worth considering when choosing a non-stick frying pan or omelette pan. Metal utensils can be used with them. Be prepared to wash up, as they are not recommended for dishwashers but are very easy to clean. Highly recommended are Meyer-Anolon.

FRYING PANS

As mentioned above, the best type of frying pan is an anodised version which is combined with a non-stick surface. The heat flexibility is insurpassable.

WOKS

Although the cheapest and best conductor of heat, carbon steel needs care and attention: namely heating, proving and wiping after use. A non-stick version, while easier to maintain, must be able to withstand the high temperatures that are necessary for stir-frying.

ROASTING TINS AND BAKING TRAYS

When you are choosing a roasting tin or baking tray, opt for something strong that won't bend and buckle. The best type is cast-iron but for a cheaper, adequate alternative, anodised aluminium is fine. A company called Mermaid produces an excellent range.

Recommended Saucepan Sizes

Size	Diameter
Large	20cm/8in
Medium	18cm/7in
Small	16cm/6½in
Very small (optional)	14cm/5in
Sauté pan	24cm/9½in
with a depth of	5cm/2in
Lidded buffet	
casserole (cast-iron)	30cm/12in
(Le Creuset terms)	

Recommended Frying Pan Sizes

Size	Diameter
Very large	26cm/10in
Small	16cm/6½in

Recommended Roasting Tin/Baking Tray Sizes

37 x 26½ x 7cm (14½ x 10½ x 2¾in)

31 x 21½ x 5cm (12½ x 8½ x 2in)

WHISKING AND MIXING

Balloon Whisks These should be springy and light. 26cm/10in in height is a good all-rounder.

Electric Hand Whisks These save on arm work! Any basic model, with two or three different speeds, will suffice.

Hand Blender This is a modern piece of kitchen equipment that has become indispensable. Excellent for puréeing and blending in anything from a saucepan to a high-sided plastic container. It is worth spending a little extra on a hand blender with a small attachment for chopping herbs and spices.

Food Processor If only one piece of electrical equipment is to be bought, it should be a good food processor. They can blend, purée, chop, slice, grate and mix all types of food. A basic size will come with various attachments and a smaller bowl. Magimix is the best value for money. Food processors last for years and save time and effort.

Kitchen Spoons Wooden spoons, metal spoons and a spider spoon (a useful wire spoon for lifting anything out of a liquid) are all useful pieces of equipment.

SMOOTHING, TURNING AND FLIPPING: SLICES AND SPATULAS

Fish Slice or Turner A fish slice or turner should be made of flexible stainless steel. It is useful for many purposes, particularly lifting and turning hot food.

Spatula Flexible metal/stainless steel long, thin spatulas are very handy for turning or lifting and moving hot foods. Plastic bowl-scrapers/spatulas are essential for scraping and clearing bowls.

Kitchen Tongs Stainless steel spring tongs are the best for turning food. Longer versions are essential for barbecues.

CUTTING, SCRAPING AND GRATING

Knives These are probably the most important component of your kitchen equipment. A good set of high-quality stainless steel knives will transform your culinary life. It is worth spending as much as you can on three or four basic knives, then building up your collection gradually. Those we recommend to start you

How to chop an onion

1 Cut in half through the root.

2 Slice vertically along the grain of the onion, but without cutting through the root.

3 Carefully holding on to the root end, make one or two horizontal cuts through the body of the onion.

4 Finally, slice against the grain, towards the core, to chop the onion into small pieces.

off are a bread/carving knife and three other knives: a cook's knife (20cm/8in), a paring knife (10cm/4in) and a serrated palette knife which has the advantage of being dual-use. Keep your knives sharp with a sharpener/steel or else a simple task will become a real chore. Excessive pressure is exerted when knives are blunt and this can be dangerous.

Graters A medium-size box stainless steel grater (four-sided) is the best.

Chopping Boards Wooden chopping boards are ever popular and adequately do the job they are meant to do. However, they do warp easily and eventually crack. Plastic polyethylene chopping boards, although not as good looking, are readily available and preferred by some. Try and have different chopping boards for raw meat, cooked meat and vegetables. Keep a folded damp cloth underneath to prevent the board from sliding as you work.

Zester This small piece of inexpensive kitchen equipment is extremely handy. Within moments, the zest from a whole fruit can be removed. When grated zest is needed, it is quicker to use a zester and then chop finely.

GRINDING AND MINCING

Pestle and Mortar A handy piece of reasonably priced equipment to have in your kitchen. The best types can be found in Thai or Chinese supermarkets.

Coffee Grinder Great not only for grinding coffee but spices too. It is best not to use the same grinder for your spices as for your coffee.

Pepper Mill Essential for freshly ground pepper. You should get used to using this as a seasoning in all your cooking. Wooden mills are best. Plastic are adequate although they tend to break.

Ladles Medium and small sizes are recommended.

SIEVING, DRYING AND STRAINING

Colander Never buy a plastic colander: they are a disaster waiting to happen because of their melting qualities. Stainless steel ones fitted with a stand are the best. A good medium-size colander to have is 20cm/8in.

BEAT BOTULISM!

Here are ten tips for food safety:

- Take chilled and frozen food home quickly, then transfer it to your fridge or freezer at once.
- Prepare and store raw and cooked food separately. Keep meat and fish at the bottom of your fridge.
- Get yourself a fridge thermometer and keep the coldest part of your fridge at 0–5°C/0–0.41°F.
- Check 'use-by' dates and use food within the manu- facturer's recommended period.
- Keep pets away from food – and dishes and worktops.
- Wash your hands thoroughly before preparing food, after using the bathroom or handling pets.
- Keep your kitchen clean. Wash worktops and utensils between handling food to be cooked and food to be served raw.
- Do not eat food containing uncooked eggs. The young, the elderly, pregnant women or anyone with immune- deficiency diseases in particular should avoid both raw or lightly cooked eggs. Although these days salmonella is very rare in eggs, always buy those stamped with the Lion Code of Practice. Keep eggs in the fridge – or below 20°C/68°F.
- Cook food well. Follow the instructions on the packet and if you reheat anything, make sure it's piping hot.
- Keep hot foods hot and cold foods cold. Don't just leave them standing around.

Sieves It is useful to have one plastic sieve, along with one metal. The plastic sieve is best for cold sauces.

Salad Spinner Most supermarkets now sell these. They are essential to ensure that washed salad leaves are completely dry.

MEASURING

Scales Digital scales are particularly efficient as any measuring bowl can be instantly incorporated into the required weight. Being plastic, they are also easy to keep clean. Traditional scales will suffice, however.

Measuring Jugs and Spoons Small/medium plastic jugs are best as the glass variety tend to chip and break. Measuring spoons can often make preparation a little easier and quicker.

MISCELLANEOUS PIECES

Tin Opener Prices of tin openers vary enormously but the cheap ones do the job just as efficiently.

Corkscrew There are many different varieties of corkscrew available and it's really up to you to choose the one with which you are most comfortable. One piece of advice: the cheap 'levered' ones can break easily.

Pyrex Bowls Recommended sizes for these heatproof bowls are: 28cm (11in), 18cm (7in) and 15cm (6in).

Ice Cream Scoop Serving ice cream is easier with a metal scoop as they retain heat when dipped in hot water.

Masher/Ricer A stainless steel masher is a good option. For a finer purée, opt for a stainless steel ricer, which resembles a very large garlic press.

Kitchen Timer Essential when you have a few things on the go! Although they require a battery, digital ones are far more reliable and accurate.

Potato Peeler Good Grips, a small kitchen equipment company, have designed an infallible version of the potato peeler. It is made of stainless steel and has a sturdy rubber grip. There are two types generally available: one is called a swivel and the other is a 'Y' peeler.

Here's our suggested list for your larder:
- Salt: Maldon is far superior to table salt
- Pepper: black, whole peppercorns
- Dried pasta: spaghetti, linguini, penne, tagliatelle
- Rice: Basmati, Carnaroli
- Couscous
- Tinned tomatoes
- Tomato purée
- Sun-dried tomatoes in oil
- Nuts: pine nuts, flaked almonds
- Pesto sauce (fine for emergencies although fresh is better)
- Soy sauce, oyster sauce, fish sauce
- Black olives (preferably bought from a good deli). Although store cupboard, these aren't for your larder. Keep them in the fridge.

Small Plastic Mandolin A cheap but handy piece of equipment designed to produce perfectly uniform slices.

LOADING UP THE LARDER

Keep a well-stocked larder. Good-quality, basic ingredients, such as oils, vinegars, herbs, spices and mustards, are an essential part of cooking good food and all can be easily stored. They are also readily available and if you don't have the inclination to buy them all in one go, take your time in choosing what really appeals to you. Most of what we suggest is readily available in supermarkets, but remember that you really can't beat quality products. Sometimes it's worth paying out that little bit extra for something that will make all the difference to a recipe – a splash of extra virgin olive oil over freshly grilled fish takes your dish to another level. And no recipe is complete without its seasoning. Maldon salt and freshly ground pepper are essential. We cannot emphasize enough the importance of tasting your food as you cook and seasoning accordingly.

HERBS AND SPICES

Herbs are a very important part of cooking. If your fingers are feeling green, grow your own herbs and then you'll always have them when you need them. They'll be fresher than the packaged or bunched type from supermarkets – and cheaper! Alternatively, find a good greengrocer to supply you with fresh, good sized bunches of herbs.

Dried herbs are fine and they do have their uses. Be careful to adapt the quantity in recipes as the drying process concentrates their flavour. You'll need considerably less than fresh.

Obviously, if you're growing herbs they'll be in your garden or on your window sill. Shop-bought fresh herbs should be purchased as needed and kept in the fridge to retain freshness.

Spices are easy to keep. They just sit in the cupboard and last for six months to two years in an airtight container. Buy them loose and whole, as spices which you can grind as needed are far superior to preground. That doesn't mean that you shouldn't attempt to cook dishes using spices if you can't get hold of whole ones. The small quantities in jars that you can buy everywhere are more than adequate, and cheap.

- Parmesan cheese (preferably bought in block form and definitely stored wrapped in your fridge)
- Flours: plain, corn, arrowroot
- Oils: olive oil, extra virgin olive oil, sunflower
- Good-quality mayonnaise
- Vinegars: red wine, white wine, good balsamic
- Mustards: Dijon, whole grain, English
- Dried mushrooms: morels, porcini
- Worcester sauce
- Good-quality chocolate – at least 65% cocoa butter
- Sugar: caster, dark muscovado
- Marigold vegetable granules
- Pink peppercorns: these have an unusual sweet flavour.

The dried herbs that we suggest you keep in your larder are:
- Oregano
- Thyme
- Rosemary
- Fennel seeds

We suggest the following spices for your larder:
- Medium curry paste
- Chilli powder
- Cumin seeds
- Saffron
- Coriander seeds
- Cardamom pods
- Paprika
- Tandoori paste
- Whole nutmeg

a lads' night in

When it comes to cooking for friends

most people would opt for the standard take-away Indian or Chinese. Well, why not break with tradition and seriously impress your friends by cooking for them? Cooking for a crowd doesn't mean that you need to be tied up in the kitchen for hours, surrounded by endless pots and pans – most of the recipes in this chapter can be cooked in one large pan. Try to use good-quality ingredients which should be available in one trip to the supermarket or by online order as this will put you ahead before you have even started. Have some sort of game plan as you don't want to be in the kitchen while the match is on!

CHICKEN CURRY

Our version of a chicken curry is very simple and speedy. Admittedly, you will not be spending many hours gathering and grinding spices, but we thought you would have better things to do. Although this recipe limits the amount of time normally spent on a curry, it certainly doesn't compromise on the taste. If you haven't got a grinder or pestle and mortar for the spices, simply substitute with preground. You can later reheat the curry, but be careful not to overcook the meat as it will become dry and stringy.

Utensils Medium saucepan or ovenproof casserole and coffee grinder or pestle and mortar

Large knob of butter
1 medium onion, chopped
18 chicken thighs, boned, skinned and cut into 4

1 If you are going to use the oven rather than the hob, preheat it to 180°C/350°F/Gas 4. Melt the butter in the saucepan or ovenproof casserole over medium heat and when it starts to foam, add the chopped onion and cook until softened. Add the chicken pieces, turning to ensure that they are well sealed all over.

2 tablespoons coriander seeds (or use preground)
2 tablespoons cumin seeds (or use preground)
4 tablespoons medium curry paste
2 x 400g/14oz tins chopped tomatoes
Salt and freshly ground black pepper

2 Prepare the spices if grinding and add them to the pan with the curry paste. Stir for a couple of minutes to enhance the flavours of the spices, then stir in the tomatoes and season. Bring to a simmer, cover and cook in the oven or on the hob over a medium heat for 25 minutes. (While the curry is cooking, use the time to prepare the rice or any other accompaniments.)

45g/1½oz fresh coriander, chopped
5cm/2in piece of creamed coconut from a 200g/7oz block

3 When the chicken has cooked (it should be firm), stir in the chopped coriander and creamed coconut. Once the coconut has melted and the coriander wilted, check the seasoning. The chicken curry is then ready to be served.

To Serve:
Cucumber Raita (page 39), naan bread, mango chutney and Basmati Rice (page 120)

4 Serve accompanied by Cucumber Raita, naan bread, mango chutney and Basmati Rice.

COURGETTE RISOTTO

As with all risottos, it's easier to have all the prepared ingredients to hand before starting to cook. We find that Carnaroli rice is the best as it keeps its shape. Remember to stir the risotto continually to make it rich and creamy. A risotto should always be finished off at the last minute with Parmesan and flavourings.

Utensils Large deep saucepan or a wok and large saucepan

450g/1lb courgettes

1 Slice away each end of the courgettes and then cut them in half. Then slice off the four long 'sides' to leave you with what is effectively a seeded cube, which you can discard. Cut the four long 'sides' into ½cm/¼in lengths and again into ½cm/¼in cubes.

50g/2oz unsalted butter
1 medium onion, chopped
2 litres/3½ pints chicken stock

2 Melt the butter in a large saucepan or wok over a medium heat and add the onion. Cook until soft. Pour the stock into a medium saucepan and bring to a gentle simmer. It's important to maintain the same heat for the stock throughout the cooking process so that when it is added to the rice, it continues to cook the rice evenly.

400g/14oz Carnaroli risotto rice

3 Add the rice to the saucepan with the butter and onions and stir continuously for a few seconds. Gradually add the stock into the rice and stir until it has been absorbed. Continue to stir, adding each ladle of stock gradually. This should take roughly 20 minutes depending on the rice. The rice can be left halfway through the cooking process and finished off nearer to the eating time. Test the rice: it should be soft but still hold its shape. It should have a little bite to it, but if it's still hard in the middle, add more stock and continue to cook.

110g/4oz Parmesan cheese, grated
3 tablespoons fresh pesto or ½ x 120g/4½oz tub
Salt and freshly ground black pepper

4 When the rice is ready, add the Parmesan cheese and courgettes with one or two more ladles of stock and cook for 1 minute more. At the end of cooking the risotto should be quite runny but the courgettes will still be crunchy. Add the pesto and seasoning, and more stock if necessary.

To Serve:
50g/2oz additional Parmesan cheese for shavings, to garnish
Rocket Salad (page 95)

5 To serve, spoon into warmed shallow bowls and garnish with Parmesan shavings. Serve with a Rocket Salad.

SHEPHERD'S PIE

An authentic Shepherd's Pie is made with minced lamb, which should be good quality and not too fatty. However, beef can be used as an alternative. For a slight difference, try a puréed root vegetable, such as swede, sweet potato or parsnip, instead of potato.

Utensils Large saucepan, large frying or sauté pan, 1 x 30cm/12in large ovenproof dish and a masher or ricer

1.35kg/3lb Maris Piper or White potatoes
1 teacup/8 fl oz milk
75g/3oz butter

1 Peel and halve the potatoes (if large) and place in a large saucepan of cold, salted water. Bring to the boil, reduce the heat and simmer for 20–25 minutes. Measure out the milk and butter to add when the potatoes are cooked.

2 medium onions
A little vegetable oil
1kg/2lb 4oz minced lamb
400g/14oz tinned chopped tomatoes
5 tablespoons tomato ketchup
8 tablespoons Worcester sauce
2 dessertspoons fennel seeds
Salt and freshly ground black pepper

2 Meanwhile, chop the onions and fry in a little oil in the large frying or sauté pan. When the onions are lightly browned, add the meat and stir thoroughly. Add the tomatoes, ketchup, Worcester sauce and fennel seeds; season well. Cook for 15 minutes or until the sauce has thickened slightly.

3 Drain the potatoes, put them back in the pan and allow to steam for a few seconds. Mash well, then add the milk and butter with plenty of seasoning. Make sure all the lumps have been removed. Pour the meat mixture into an ovenproof dish, cover evenly with mash and mark with a fork to decorate. (At this stage the pie, when cooled, can be wrapped with clingfilm and kept in the fridge. The meat should be cooled as quickly as possible if you are going to reheat it later.)

To Serve:
Cumin Beans (page 116) or a green salad

4 Preheat the oven to 200°C/400°F/Gas 6. Bake the pie for 20 minutes while preparing an accompanying vegetable or salad. If reheating, add 5 minutes to the baking time.

Top Man Tip Different flavourings can be added to mash (pages 33, 51, 106–7, 120 and 121).

KEDGEREE

Kedgeree originated as a breakfast dish for the British Colonialists in India and it is equally popular now as a supper dish. We use mushrooms and fresh fish, as well as smoked fish, to give it a lighter texture and fresher taste.

Utensils 2 large frying pans or large ovenproof dish, coffee grinder or pestle and mortar, 1 medium saucepan and 1 small saucepan

350g/12oz smoked haddock fillet
350g/12oz fresh haddock fillet
A few black peppercorns
1 bay leaf
Salt and freshly ground black pepper

1 Preheat the oven to 180°C/350°F/Gas 4. First poach the fish by placing the fillets skin-side up in a frying pan or ovenproof dish. Cover with boiling water, add the peppercorns and bay leaf; bring to a simmer. Then cover with foil and put in the oven for 15 minutes or until the skin of the fish is easy to remove. Take the fish out of the water and leave to cool.

Curry Sauce:
50g/2oz butter
1 medium onion, chopped
1 clove garlic
1 teaspoon cumin seeds
¼ teaspoon fennel seeds
1 teaspoon tomato purée
1 teaspoon turmeric
1 teaspoon curry powder
Large pinch of saffron
1 bay leaf
150ml/¼ pint cold water

2 To make the curry sauce, melt the butter and gently fry the chopped onion in a large frying pan or ovenproof dish over a low heat. Crush the garlic, grind the cumin and fennel seeds (if using whole seeds) and add to the pan to fry for 3 minutes. Add the tomato purée, turmeric, curry powder, saffron, bay leaf and water, then simmer for 15 minutes, uncovered.

300g/11oz Basmati Rice (page 120)
1 teaspoon cumin seeds

3 While the sauce is cooking, prepare the Basmati Rice with the addition of the cumin seeds.

350g/12oz chestnut mushrooms
3 medium eggs

4 Flake the fish fillets into large chunks and remove any bones, skin, peppercorns and the bay leaf. Chop the mushrooms into quarters and boil the eggs. To do this, cover the eggs with cold water in a saucepan, bring to the boil and simmer for 6 minutes. Immerse in very cold running water until cool, then peel and cut.

50g/2oz butter
15g/¾oz flat leaf parsley, chopped

5 To serve, reheat the curry sauce over a gentle heat and add the mushrooms, stirring well to cook (about 3–4 minutes). Carefully stir in the delicate fish and rice; heat well through for 4–5 minutes (the rice should be over 65°C/149°F). Season and add the remaining butter. Place the eggs on top, scatter with parsley and spoon onto hot plates.

CHILLI CON CARNE

This recipe can be cooked, chilled and reheated later on. As with any recipe using tinned beans, be sure to rinse the kidney beans well before use. This chilli dish has just a few added seasonings which we think make all the difference. Don't buy supermarket olives as they are often tasteless. Instead, try a good deli. Olives can be stored, sealed, in the fridge for a few weeks.

Utensils Coffee grinder or pestle and mortar, small bowl, large, shallow saucepan or wok

3 tablespoons cumin seeds (or use preground)
2 tablespoons each chilli powder, Dijon mustard, dried basil and dried oregano

1 Grind the cumin if using whole seeds, then place it in a bowl with the chilli powder, Dijon mustard, dried basil and dried oregano. Keep to one side.

2 medium onions
1 clove garlic
A little vegetable oil
900g/2lb minced beef

2 Chop the onions and garlic and fry in a little oil in a large saucepan or wok until soft. Add the meat and fry gently for 3–4 minutes. Add the dried herb and spice mixture and cook for a further 3 minutes.

2 x 400g/14oz tins chopped tomatoes
2 tablespoons tomato purée
1 teacup red wine
1 medium lemon, juiced
Salt and freshly ground black pepper

3 Add the tomatoes, tomato purée, red wine and lemon juice. Stir well and bring to a simmer. Season and continue to cook gently, uncovered, for 15 minutes.

400g/14oz tin red kidney beans, well rinsed
2 tablespoons dried dill
30g/1¼oz flat leaf parsley, chopped
275g/10oz pitted black olives

4 Add the kidney beans, dill, chopped parsley and olives. Simmer gently, uncovered, for a further 15 minutes. Check the seasoning and serve with Cornbread or rice.

To Serve:
Cornbread (page 24)

Top Man Tip Whenever you cook with spices, make sure that you allow them enough time in the first stages of cooking to 'cook out'. This will give the dish a superior flavour and remove any bitterness from the raw spices.

FAJITAS

Fajita actually describes the 'skirt steak', the cut of beef originally eaten by the ranch hands in Northern Mexico and Texas. The dish is a Tex-Mex phenomenon although fajitas do not actually exist in Mexico. Although there are many ready-made ingredients now available, try this home-made fresh, light version and you will never go back. Everything is simple to whip up and it can all be prepared (apart from the chicken) beforehand. A fajita is a variation on a taco using a soft tortilla. These days different fillings can be used. Beef, fish or prawns can be substituted for the chicken or add extra onions or peppers according to taste. For a change, try dried chillies, which can be soaked in boiling water and puréed.

Utensils Food processor or blender, plastic or china bowls, baking tray, lidded saucepan (optional), heatproof Pyrex bowl, large ovenproof dish, serving bowls and large frying pan and grater

6 boneless, skinless chicken breasts
¼ teacup olive oil
2 tablespoons dried oregano
1 medium onion
2 tablespoons lemon juice
Salt and freshly ground black pepper

1 Cut the chicken breasts in half lengthways and then into thin strips. In a food processor, purée the oil, oregano, onion and lemon juice. Season. Coat the chicken strips well with the marinade in a plastic or china bowl, cover and refrigerate for as long as you can, preferably 2–4 hours.

Rajas:
3 red peppers
3 yellow peppers

2 To make the Rajas (peppers), turn the grill to its highest setting. Cut the peppers in half lengthways and remove the seeds and stalks. Put the peppers skin-side up on a baking tray and grill until the skin has blackened. Place in a plastic bag or saucepan with lid and leave to cool. The skin can then be easily pulled away. Slice the peppers into thin strips and keep to reheat later on.

Guacamole:
3 fresh green chillies
2 limes
3 ripe avocados
45g/1½oz fresh coriander

3 Deseed the chillies and juice the limes. Using either a hand blender and a bowl or food processor, blend all the Guacamole ingredients to a purée; season. Alternatively, mash the avocado in a bowl with a fork, chop the rest of the ingredients and mix them all together. This does not have to be a smooth purée.

Salsa:
450g/1lb vine tomatoes
1 small red onion
30g/1¼oz fresh coriander
2 small red chillies, fresh or dried
Juice of 2 limes
Salt and freshly ground black pepper

4 Skin the tomatoes for the Salsa by placing them in a bowl of boiling water for 1 minute. Check the skins peel away easily. Immerse in cold water. Remove the skins, cut in half horizontally and deseed using a teaspoon. Chop the tomatoes and onion into 1cm/½in squares. Roughly chop the coriander, deseed the chillies and finely chop. Mix the Salsa ingredients together in a bowl. Sprinkle with lime juice, season and gently stir. Cover and chill until needed.

5 Preheat the oven to 170°C/325°F/Gas 3. Place the peppers in an ovenproof dish and heat through for 15–20 minutes. When ready to serve, wrap the tortillas in foil and place in the oven (they will only take a few minutes to heat through).

A little vegetable oil

6 Check the Salsa and Guacamole seasoning. Pour sour cream into a serving bowl and grate the cheese into another. Heat a little oil in a frying pan and when very hot, start to fry the chicken strips in batches (this will only take about 4 minutes). As you finish each batch, keep warm in the oven.

To Serve:
12 or more ready-made flour tortillas
425ml/15 fl oz sour cream
250g/9oz Cheddar cheese, grated

7 To serve, lay the warmed tortillas flat and place some of the hot chicken and Rajas down the centre. Spoon on a little Salsa, Guacamole and sour cream. Sprinkle with grated cheese. Roll up and enjoy!

CORNBREAD

This cornbread was originally served with Chilli con Carne in the USA. It makes an interesting alternative to chilli with rice and is easy and quick to make.

Utensils Small baking tray, 2 large bowls and a small saucepan

1 teacup full fat milk
(220ml/8 fl oz)
1 tablespoon lemon juice

1 teacup cornmeal or semolina
1 teacup plain flour
3 teaspoons baking powder

80g/3oz butter
1 medium egg
4 level tablespoons sugar
Salt and freshly ground black pepper

4 tablespoons parsley
400g/14oz tin sweetcorn, drained

1 Preheat the oven to 200°C/400°F/Gas 6 and line the bottom of a baking tray with silicone/greaseproof paper. Mix the milk and lemon juice together in a large bowl.

2 In another bowl, mix together the cornmeal or semolina, flour and baking powder.

3 Melt the butter gently in a saucepan over low heat. Into the bowl containing the milk and lemon juice, add the egg, sugar and melted butter, then the flour, cornmeal, baking powder mixture and seasoning. Gently combine.

4 Chop the parsley. Add the sweetcorn and parsley to the thick creamy mixture, stir a few times and pour into the baking tray. Bake in the oven for 20–25 minutes until the cornbread is just firm. It should still have a light crumbly texture.

5 To serve, cut into large squares and eat when it's still slightly warm.

Top Man Tip A couple of chopped fresh chillies can be added for a bit of a kick.

JOHNNY VAUGHAN'S "GODFATHER MEATBALLS"

Serves 6

Preparation and Cooking Time: 45 minutes

This is one of Johnny Vaughan's favourite recipes. It is an authentic Italian dish that would be good enough for Marlon Brando.

Utensils Food processor, a large mixing bowl, frying pan and large saucepan

100g/3½oz fresh white bread (about 3 slices)
1 onion

1 In the bowl of a food processor fitted with a metal blade, blend the white bread to fine breadcrumbs. Add the onion and chop finely.

225g/8oz each of minced beef, veal and pork
1 garlic clove, crushed
2 teaspoons dried oregano
1 small handful fresh parsley, chopped
1 egg

2 Transfer to a mixing bowl and mix together well with the minced meat, garlic, oregano, parsley and egg. Use your hands to roll the mixture into 3.5cm/1½in balls.

A little plain flour and vegetable oil

3 Dust with a little flour. Heat a little oil in a frying pan and fry the meatballs lightly until golden brown.

1 onion, chopped finely
1 garlic clove, crushed
700g/1½lb passata (thick, sieved tomatoes)
150ml/¼ pint dry white wine
1 small handful fresh basil (or 2 teaspoons dried)
Salt and freshly ground black pepper

4 Preheat the oven to 180°C/350°F/Gas 4. Meanwhile, add a little oil to the frying pan and gently fry the onion and garlic together, then stir in the passata, white wine and basil. Season well. Return the meatballs to the pan and bring the sauce to a simmer. Using the same pan or an ovenproof dish, cover and bake for 30 minutes.

1.5kg/3lb 5oz dried spaghetti

To Serve:
Freshly grated Parmesan

5 While the meatballs are baking, boil a large saucepan of salted water for the spaghetti and cook for 6–8 minutes until al dente. Drain the spaghetti and serve with a good spoonful of meatballs and sauce on top and sprinkle with plenty of freshly grated Parmesan.

CHRIS EVANS' POST-PUB PASTA

Chris Evans suggests the following pasta dishes when returning home from the pub with your mates. There are three different sauces to choose from, depending on how pissed you are!

PASTA
3 handfuls of penne

1 Add the pasta to boiling salted water, reduce to a simmer and cook until the pasta turns white. Check by mouth: the pasta should be firm but not chewy. Drain in a colander.

SAUCES A choice of three, depending on your state ...

Not Too Pissed:

Knob of butter
1 onion, chopped

1 Melt the butter in a saucepan over a low heat. Add the onion and leave to sweat (the onions, not you!)

2 cloves of garlic, chopped
Salt and freshly ground black pepper
Pinch of sugar
½ tin chopped tomatoes

2 Add the garlic, seasoning and sugar, followed by the tomatoes. Stir and leave to simmer.

Half a round of Boursin cheese
1 dessertspoon green pesto

3 Add the Boursin cheese and pesto. Stir and continue to simmer.

3 splashes red wine

4 Add the red wine and continue to simmer.

Handful grated Cheddar cheese

5 Turn up the heat and add the Cheddar until it all starts bubbling.

6 When the cheese has melted, take the pan off the heat and mix the sauce with the drained pasta. Serve immediately.

Pretty Pissed:

Knob of butter
1 onion, chopped
1 clove garlic, chopped

1 Over a low heat, melt the butter in a pan. Add the onion, followed by the garlic and gently fry.

1 glass of wine or more
Salt and freshly ground black pepper
Pinch of sugar
Tin tuna, drained

2 Add the wine, seasoning and sugar. Stir in the tuna.

½ glass tomato juice

3 Add the tomato juice. Stir and simmer. Add more wine if you like – the longer you simmer, the tastier it'll be!

4   Take the pan off the heat and mix the sauce with the drained pasta. Serve immediately.

Very Pissed:

1   Have the pasta already cooked and drained in a colander.

Knob of butter   **2**   Melt the butter in a saucepan over low heat. Remove from the heat.

2–3 dribbles of olive oil
Mouthful of white wine
Generous sprinkling of
Parmesan cheese

3   Stir in the olive oil and wine. Return to the heat and add the pasta and Parmesan cheese.

4   Place the lid back on the saucepan, remove from the heat and shake it.

1 egg
Salt and freshly ground black
pepper

5   Remove the lid, break the egg over the pasta, season, mix together and serve immediately.

NB: For cooking times, just guess.

norman no mates

(and his brother, Scot)

Cooking for one doesn't have to be a chore.

It won't entail too much effort and it'll make a welcome change from heating up something in a cheap, plastic container. Most of the following recipes use fresh ingredients that can be bought at convenience stores or corner shops on the way home from work and simply added to shop-bought or pre-packaged foods. You can then have a very tasty and satisfying dinner in very little time.

PAPPARDELLE WITH FENNEL, PRAWNS AND TOMATO SAUCE

Serves 1

Preparation and Cooking Time:

25 minutes

You can change the pasta for this dish, but the prawns should be raw and preferably with their heads still on to obtain the freshest and finest taste. Try to avoid the watery and frozen types now available in the supermarkets – they are tasteless and a waste of money.

Utensils 1 medium, deep saucepan and 1 medium saucepan

1 small knob of butter
½ onion, chopped

1 Begin to boil the salted water for the pasta in a large, deep saucepan. Melt the butter and sweat the onions in a medium saucepan until they are just beginning to brown.

150g/5oz tinned chopped tomatoes
60ml/2 fl oz white wine
¼ dessertspoon fennel seeds
½ dessertspoon tomato purée
Salt and freshly ground black pepper

2 Add the tomatoes, white wine, fennel seeds and tomato purée. Simmer gently for 5–10 minutes, or until the tomatoes reduce to a thick sauce. Season.

110g/4oz pappardelle, dried
¼ fennel bulb, thinly sliced

3 Add the pasta to the pan of water, reduce the heat and simmer for 6–10 minutes. Add the sliced fennel to the simmering tomato sauce.

125g/4¼oz raw tiger prawns, preferably with heads on

4 Add the shelled prawns to the sauce and season again. Simmer for 3–4 minutes until the prawns are firm and turn pink.

5 Drain the pasta through a colander and mix with the sauce in the pasta pan.

To Serve:
Freshly grated Parmigiano Reggiano (Parmesan cheese)

6 Serve in a warmed bowl with freshly grated Parmesan cheese sprinkled on top.

Top Man Tip It is well worth spending a little extra on a good-quality dried pasta. When cooked, it should still be 'al dente' (have a little bite).

MACARONI CHEESE WITH HAM

This is always popular as a quick pasta dish and is a good recipe to have in your standard repertoire. The recipe uses a supermarket-based sauce but when Mascarpone and extra Parmesan cheeses are added, it soon becomes rich and tasty. Try it with different pasta shapes.

Utensils 2 medium saucepans and a medium ovenproof dish

Small knob of butter
½ medium onion, chopped

1   Preheat the oven to 200°C/400°F/Gas 6. Melt the butter in a medium saucepan, add the onion and fry gently for a few minutes. Meanwhile, boil a medium saucepan of salted water for the macaroni.

4 heaped tablespoons ready-made cheese sauce or cheese pasta sauce
4 heaped tablespoons Mascarpone cheese
25g/1oz Parmigiano Reggiano, grated plus 15g/¾oz Parmesan cheese, grated
Salt and freshly ground black pepper

2   Stir in the cheese sauce, Mascarpone and Parmesan cheeses with the onions over a gentle heat and season.

175g/6oz macaroni
50g/2oz cooked ham, thickly sliced or in pieces
1 handful flat leaf parsley, chopped

3   Add the macaroni to the boiling water and simmer for 10 minutes. Chop the ham into 2cm/¾in cubes and add it to the sauce with the parsley.

4   When the macaroni has cooked, drain and mix it into the sauce. Season well.

5   Pour into an ovenproof serving dish. Sprinkle with the rest of the Parmesan cheese. Place the dish in the middle of the hot oven for 10 minutes. When cooked, it should be golden on top.

To Serve:
Green herb salad (pre-prepared)

6   Serve in a warmed bowl with a green herb salad.

Top Man Tip   Large mixed chunks of ham or gammon can be purchased from most supermarket deli counters. These are the cut ends of whole hams.

PORK SAUSAGES IN ONION AND HERB GRAVY

Serves 1

Preparation and Cooking Time:
40 minutes

This recipe is perfect for that special winter evening treat when you have a little more time on your hands. Multiply the quantities and it is also perfect for cooking for a crowd, although go easy on the garlic!

Utensils Medium ovenproof frying pan with lid, 1 medium saucepan, small baking tray and potato masher

Small knob of butter
200g/7oz pork and herb sausages (or about 4)
225g/8oz onions, sliced thinly

1 Preheat the oven to 190°C/375°F/Gas 5. Melt the butter in a medium frying pan and fry the sausages on a low heat until they start to brown. After 5 minutes, take them out. Replace with the onion and fry for another 5–10 minutes or until coloured and soft.

350g/12 oz white potatoes

2 Peel the potatoes and cut them into large chunks. Cover with cold, salted water in a medium saucepan, bring to the boil and simmer until soft, about 20–25 minutes.

150ml/¼ pint boiling water
150ml/¼ pint red wine
½ tablespoon chopped thyme
Salt and freshly ground black pepper

3 Add the boiling water, red wine and thyme to the onions in the same frying pan. Bring to the boil. Season well and add the sausages. When simmering, put the lid on the pan and bake in the oven for 30 minutes.

3 large cloves garlic (leave whole with peel on)

4 Meanwhile, put the garlic cloves on a baking tray. Place on the top shelf of the oven and bake for 15 minutes.

Knob of butter
3 tablespoons milk

5 Test the potatoes with a sharp knife. When soft, drain and put back in the same pan. Leave to steam for a few seconds. Mash well and then add the butter and milk. Cut the ends away from the garlic cloves and squeeze out the soft, baked insides. Add to the mash, mash well and season. Keep warm in the same pan with the lid on, or cover with clingfilm.

1 teaspoon arrowroot
1 tablespoon cold water

6 Remove the sausages from the oven. To thicken the liquid, put the pan on a low heat to simmer and stir in the arrowroot mixed with cold water. Leave to simmer and thicken. Taste and season again.

Top Man Tips Arrowroot thickens clear sauces well. If you can't get hold of it, try cornflour. And don't cut the potatoes into too small pieces or the mash will be very watery.

THAI CHICKEN STIR FRY

This is a quick and simple dish that is easy to prepare when you get in late from work. A little added effort makes all the difference to using a pre-made stir fry sauce. If you're serving this with rice, start to prepare it at the same time as the chicken.

Utensils Wok

1 clove garlic
2.5cm/1in piece fresh ginger
1 stick lemongrass
½ red chilli

1 Peel the garlic and ginger and grate. Cut the lemongrass in half lengthways and slice very finely. Remove the seeds from the chilli and chop finely. Mix the ingredients together.

1½ tablespoons each: dark soy sauce and rice wine vinegar
1 tablespoon sunflower oil
Salt and freshly ground black pepper

2 Add the soy, vinegar and sunflower oil; season.

1 medium chicken breast
110g/4oz shiitake mushrooms

3 Cut the chicken breast in half lengthways. Then diagonally slice into 1cm/½in strips. Slice the shiitake mushrooms into ½cm/¼in slices. (If serving with accompaniments, cook these before you begin stir-frying.)

A little extra sunflower oil

4 Heat the wok until smoking and add a little oil. Add the chicken and season, turning occasionally with a spatula for approximately 1 minute. Add the chilli mix and mushrooms. Cook for a further 3–4 minutes or until the mushrooms feel soft and the chicken is firm. Serve with Asian Greens or rice.

To Serve:
Asian Greens (page 96) or rice

Top Man Tip When buying lemongrass, make sure the sticks are fresh, firm and not dried-looking. If necessary, the outer leaves can be peeled away to reveal a fresh inner core.

MONKFISH STIR FRY WITH OYSTER SAUCE

You can supplement this dish with a bag of shop-bought, fresh stir-fry vegetables but for a better result, cut the vegetables yourself into a more uniform size. For this dish, the fish must be as fresh as you can find as older fish will disintegrate as soon as you start cooking. The oyster sauce, despite its name, doesn't taste fishy. It has a rich flavour which goes well with fish and most stir-fry dishes. Widely available bottled, it is best kept refrigerated after opening.

Utensils Wok

1cm/½in piece fresh ginger
½ clove garlic
150g/5oz monkfish

1 As with all stir-fries, it is essential to prepare the ingredients before you start to cook. Grate the ginger (leave the skin on if you want), crush the garlic and cut the monkfish into 4 x 2cm/1½ x ¾in strips, ensuring the membrane has been removed (see Top Man Tip).

½ medium Chinese leaf lettuce
½ carrot
4 spring onions
½ red pepper

2 Cut lengthways through the root and then thinly slice the Chinese leaf. Cut the carrot into matchstick strips and slice the spring onions diagonally and thinly. After removing the seeds and stalk from the red pepper, cut it into 4 x ½cm/2 x ¼in strips.

1 tablespoon sunflower oil
¼ bottle oyster sauce (about 4 tablespoons)
Salt and freshly ground black pepper

3 Heat the wok over a high heat and add the oil, garlic and ginger. Only when it is very hot, add the fish, stirring continuously. After a few seconds, add the vegetables. This will only take 3–4 minutes to cook. When the lettuce has wilted slightly, add the oyster sauce; stir and heat through, then add the seasoning.

To Serve:
Braised Mushrooms
(page 112)

Serve immediately with Braised Mushrooms.

Top Man Tip When cooking monkfish, remember that after the skin has been removed there is a second thin skin which should also come off before cooking.

QUICK PIZZA

For the best results, pizzas should be prepared from scratch and then baked in a stone oven. This alternative is not quite as authentic but it certainly beats the plastic variety found in supermarkets. The hot baking tray heats the pizza from the bottom to make it crispy.

Utensils Large and medium saucepans and large, flat baking tray

700g/1½lb plum tomatoes

1 To peel the tomatoes, place them in a large saucepan and cover with boiling water. Leave for 1 minute and check that the skin peels away easily. Pour away the hot water and immerse the tomatoes in cold water. Peel off the skins and discard. Cut the tomatoes in half horizontally and use a teaspoon to remove the seeds. Roughly chop all the tomatoes.

Olive oil for frying
1 onion, chopped
1 clove garlic
Salt and freshly ground black pepper

2 Add a little oil to a medium saucepan and cook the onion over a medium heat. Add the garlic, then the chopped tomatoes. Season and cook gently for a few minutes until slightly soft. Preheat the oven to 220°C/425°F/Gas 7 and put the baking tray in to heat.

110g/4oz goats cheese
200g/7oz Buffalo mozzarella
2 teaspoons Pesto, in a jar or freshly made
2 tablespoons olive oil

3 Cut the goats cheese into small pieces and slice the mozzarella. Mix the pesto with 2 tablespoons olive oil.

Large (approximately 29cm/11½in) thick ready-made pizza base
50g/2oz pitted olives

4 Place the pizza base on the hot baking tray, cover with the tomato mixture and place the cheese and olives on top. Drizzle with pesto oil and season well. Bake the pizza in the oven for 10 minutes or until brown.

To Serve:
Fresh basil

5 To serve, slice and serve on a warm plate. Garnish with fresh basil.

PENNE WITH ROASTED TOMATO SAUCE AND GREMOLATA

Serves 1

Preparation and Cooking Time:

25 minutes

Roasting a tomato gives an added caramelised flavour to this recipe which is quite unique. The gremolata can add a little extra zing to any tomato-based dish.

Utensils Large saucepan, large baking tray, zester, small mixing bowl and hand blender or food processor

225g/8oz plum or vine tomatoes
A little olive oil
Salt and freshly ground black pepper

1 Boil a large saucepan of salted water for the pasta. Preheat the oven to 200°C/400°F/Gas 6. Halve the tomatoes, leaving the skin on. Place on a baking tray, cut side up. Drizzle with olive oil and add plenty of seasoning. Roast near the top of the oven for 20 minutes. When cooked, the edges of the tomatoes should caramelise to add to the flavour.

Gremolata:
½ medium lemon
½ clove garlic, chopped
1 handful fresh flat leaf parsley, chopped
Salt and freshly ground black pepper

2 Meanwhile, using a zester, zest the lemon and in a small bowl, mix it with the chopped garlic, parsley and seasoning.

150g/5oz penne pasta

3 Add the pasta to the boiling water and cook for 8–10 minutes. The pasta should have a slight bite: be careful not to overcook it.

4 Meanwhile, blend the tomatoes with a hand blender or food processor. Taste to check seasoning. Cover to keep warm (clingfilm may be used). Drain the pasta, pour it back into the empty pan and drizzle with a little olive oil, salt and pepper.

5 Pour the pasta immediately onto a hot plate. Top with the tomato sauce and sprinkle a little Gremolata on top.

Top Man Tip Gremolata is usually served with Osso Bucco, a rich tomato-based Italian braised veal dish. The lemon rind could be replaced with orange.

Serves 1
Preparation and Cooking Time:
25 minutes
(and marinading overnight)

TANDOORI CHICKEN

This is a simple spicy dish that can be prepared a day in advance and cooked in a matter of minutes. Along with a little Cucumber Raita (opposite), it makes a great fast recipe when you get in late from work.

Utensils Coffee grinder or pestle and mortar, small bowl, container to hold chicken breasts and small baking tray or ovenproof dish

Marinade:
1 teaspoon each cumin and coriander seeds (or preground)
6 teaspoons tandoori paste
150g/5oz natural yoghurt
Salt and freshly ground black pepper

1 If you are not using preground spices, grind the cumin and coriander seeds for the marinade in a coffee grinder or small blender or pestle and mortar. Mix together the tandoori paste, yoghurt and ground spices in a small bowl; season.

1 or 2 medium chicken breasts

2 Put the chicken breast(s) in a container with sides and pierce the skin with a sharp knife. Pour over the tandoori mix, turn to coat and cover. Leave to marinade in the fridge as long as possible, preferably overnight.

3 Preheat the oven to 200°C/400°F/Gas 6. Transfer the chicken to a small baking tray or ovenproof dish, spacing each piece well apart. Season. Cook for 20 minutes at the top of the oven.

To Serve:
Basmati Rice (page 120), chopped coriander; mango chutney and Cucumber Raita (page 39)

4 Serve the chicken with Basmati Rice with chopped coriander forked through. You can also serve mango chutney and Cucumber Raita.

Top Man Tip This is also a great dish for barbecuing.

CUCUMBER RAITA

This is an easy-to-make, refreshing accompaniment to most Asian dishes.

Utensils Medium sized bowl

1 cucumber

1 Peel and halve the cucumber lengthways. Remove the seeds with a teaspoon and cut into 1cm/½in cubes.

1 small bunch mint (about 15g/¾oz)
150g/5oz natural yoghurt
Salt and freshly ground black pepper

2 Chop the mint and mix all the ingredients together in a bowl. Season and serve chilled.

BAKED BEANS ON FOCACCIA

Tinned baked beans are still one of the best fast foods. This recipe just gives a Bloody Mary twist, minus the vodka! The focaccia is perfect for toasting.

Utensils Small saucepan

420g/14½oz tin baked beans

1 Pour the beans into the small saucepan and heat through gently.

2 teaspoons horseradish sauce (not creamed)
2 tablespoons Worcester sauce
Salt and freshly ground black pepper

2 Stir in the horseradish and Worcester sauces while heating, then season.

1 focaccia

3 Toast 1 or 2 thick slices of focaccia under the grill.

4 To serve, transfer the toast to a large plate. Season the beans with salt and pepper. Pour them over the toast and eat.

chapter four

brownie points

(or, how to titillate her tastebuds)

Fact: wining and dining lead to romance.

Organising dinner at a fancy restaurant is one way to impress but another, far more original way to reach a woman's heart is through your own kitchen. Not only will you be able to choose a menu to suit your date's particular taste but you will also be able to set the scene to suit you. Don't feel you have to cook to impress – cooking at home is all about working at your own pace and attempting dishes that you are comfortable with.

ROASTED SALMON WITH PEPPER SALSA

This is a light dish with a refreshing, piquant pepper salsa. Try to buy organically farmed or wild salmon as it has a far superior flavour.

Utensils Baking tray, 2 bowls (1 heatproof) and frying pan

2 red peppers, halved and deseeded

1 For the salsa, preheat the grill to its highest setting. Place the peppers, skin side up, on the baking tray and put them under the grill. They will be ready when the skin has blackened. Peel and cut into 1cm/½in squares (see Top Man Tip).

2 medium vine or plum tomatoes

2 Peel the tomatoes by placing them in a bowl and pour boiling water over them. Leave for 1 minute, check the skins come away easily, then transfer to a bowl of very cold water. Cut them in half, remove the seeds with a teaspoon and cut into 1cm/½in cubes.

½ red onion
15g/¾oz fresh coriander
15g/¾oz flat leaf parsley

3 Finely chop the red onion and roughly chop the coriander and parsley.

½ medium lemon, juiced
½ medium lime, juiced
2 tablespoons olive oil
Salt and freshly ground black pepper

4 Mix all the chopped ingredients in a bowl with the lemon and lime juices and olive oil. Season well. (You can make the salsa a little in advance as the flavours will mature.)

2 x 150g/5oz salmon fillets (preferably organically farmed)
Salt and freshly ground black pepper
Small knob of butter

5 Preheat the oven to 200°C/400°F/Gas 6. Season the salmon and melt the butter in a frying pan over a medium heat. As the butter foams, add the salmon skin-side down. Leave for 3 minutes then place the pan and its contents in the oven for approximately 7 minutes. Once cooked, the salmon should still be moist in the middle – check using a sharp knife.

To Serve:
A little chilli oil

6 Place each salmon fillet onto a plate, pile plenty of salsa on top and drizzle with a little chilli oil. Serve immediately.

Top Man Tip To ensure the pepper skins peel away easily, put them in a plastic bag or saucepan with a lid and leave to cool first before gently pulling away the skins.

RED MULLET SALTIMBOCCA

As with other fish dishes, it is very important to use fish that is as fresh as possible. If you're able to buy your fish direct from a fishmonger, he will be able to help you with scaling or boning. If you can't solicit your friendly fishmonger's help and you buy red mullet fillets that need boning and scaling, use tweezers to remove any bones down the middle of the fish fillet, feeling for them first with your finger. If the fillets aren't prescaled, scrape the skin with the back of a knife and rinse them well with cold water, then dry. When buying fresh whole fish, look for bright eyes, shiny scales and no overpowering fishy smell.

This particular dish can be prepared beforehand and fried when needed. It is an adaptation of an Italian veal recipe. The all-important part is to finish it off properly with butter and lemon to give a good, sharp taste. If red mullet is difficult to find, you could try tilapia.

Utensils Large frying pan

4 large slices of parma ham
4 red mullet fillets, 175g/6oz each
Salt and freshly ground black pepper

1 Lay a slice of parma ham on a flat work surface and place a fish fillet on top, skin side down. Season, then wrap the ham around the middle of the fillet. Repeat this procedure for all the fish fillets, cover and refrigerate until you're ready to start cooking. If you are serving the fish with anything else, prepare it before you begin frying.

4 tablespoons plain flour
4 large sage leaves

2 Pour the flour onto a large plate and season. Take each fish fillet, roll in the flour and shake off any excess. Press a sage leaf onto each fillet.

A little sunflower oil

3 Pour the oil into a large frying pan and place over a medium heat. When the pan is hot, add the fish fillets, sage side down. Fry for 2–3 minutes or until the fish is crisp, then turn over and fry for a further 2–3 minutes. (If your pan isn't big enough to fry all the fillets in one go, fry them in batches and keep them warm in a low oven [150°C/300°F/Gas 2] on a warmed serving dish.)

50g/2oz unsalted butter
1 lemon, juiced

4 When the fish is cooked, place it in the serving dish. Drain away any remaining oil and, using the same pan, melt the butter until it starts to foam. Add salt and pepper and lemon juice to the butter, warm through and pour over the crisp fillets.

To Serve:
Buttered new potatoes tossed with chopped chives, wilted spinach with nutmeg or Mushrooms en Papillote (page 108)

5 Serve with buttered new potatoes tossed with chopped chives, and wilted spinach with nutmeg, or Mushrooms en Papillote. (All of these side dishes can be cooked in advance and kept warm in a low oven [150°C/300°F/Gas 2] while you finish the fish.)

THAI BAKED SKATE

Any fish could be substituted for the skate we use here. You could try monkfish, cod or John Dory. Steam cooking with Thai ingredients gives a subtle flavour rather than permeating the fish. Once you have mastered this type of steam cooking, you can cook lots of different foods in this way. Sealing in the natural juices and flavours is not only delicious, but easy to do and healthy. Try the following method with thin slices of chicken, fresh basil and cherry tomatoes or prawns with a dash of Pernod.

Utensils Grater, zester, mixing bowl, palette knife, small baking tray and fish slice (optional)

1 Preheat the oven to 190°C/375°F/Gas 5.

1 teaspoon fresh ginger
1 tablespoon fresh coriander
1 clove garlic
1 lime
1 spring onion
Salt and freshly ground black pepper

2 Leaving the skin on, grate the ginger, chop the coriander and garlic, zest and juice the lime and thinly slice the spring onion. Mix all the ingredients together in a bowl and season with salt and pepper.

2 x 175g/6oz skate wings

3 Place each skate wing on a large piece of tin foil. Divide the prepared mixture equally and, using a palette knife, spread it evenly over the skate. Season and wrap the foil securely around the fish to make a tent-like parcel.

4 Place the fish parcels on a small baking tray and bake in the oven for 20 minutes. (These can be prepared in advance of cooking.)

To Serve:
Rice and a green vegetable or stir-fried vegetables

5 To serve, place each foil parcel on a warmed plate or scoop the fish out using a fish slice, making sure all the juices are poured over. Serve with rice and a green vegetable or stir-fried vegetables. These can be prepared and then finished off when the fish goes into the oven.

CHICKEN DIJONNAISE

Although we specify chicken breasts here, you can also use pork fillet for this recipe. Cut the pork into thin slices and cook for only 5–10 minutes. Be careful not to overcook the chicken or pork as it will become stringy and tough.

Utensils Small baking tray and small saucepan

1 tablespoon grainy mustard
1 tablespoon Dijon mustard
2 chicken breasts, skinned

1 Mix the two mustards together and pierce each chicken breast a few times with a sharp knife. Spread the mustard over the chicken and leave for as long as possible, preferably 1-2 hours, covered, in the fridge. It's not imperative that the chicken is left to marinade so if you don't have the time, just go straight to the next stage.

2 Preheat the oven to 200C°/400F°/Gas 6. If you plan to serve Basmati Rice with this dish, start cooking it now.

Salt and freshly ground black pepper
150ml/¼ pint white wine

3 Place the chicken on a baking tray, season and pour over the wine. Bake in the oven for 15 minutes.

4 Remove the chicken from the oven and scrape off the mustard. Place the mustard in a small saucepan along with any chicken/wine juices. Put a piece of foil over the chicken and put it back in the oven.

3 heaped tablespoons crème fraîche

5 Stir the crème fraîche into the mustards, mix well and leave to simmer for about 5 minutes uncovered. When the sauce is ready, it will be the thickness of double cream. Check the seasoning. Any accompaniments can be finished off whilst the sauce is reducing (simmering gently to thicken).

To Serve:
Basmati Rice (page 120), wilted spinach or Cumin Beans (page 116)

6 To serve, place the chicken either whole or sliced on a warm plate and cover with the creamy mustard sauce. It is particularly good with Basmati Rice and spinach or Cumin Beans.

Serves 2

Preparation and Cooking Time:

35 minutes

RATATOUILLE WITH MERGUEZ SAUSAGES

Merguez, a spicy Algerian sausage, made with lamb and harissa, is delicious and, if available, well worth using in this recipe.

Utensils Large saucepan with lid and a large frying pan

2 tablespoons olive oil
1 onion, cut into 2cm/¾in squares
1 garlic clove, chopped
1 aubergine, cut into quarters, then into 4cm/1½in pieces
1 red pepper, cut into quarters, deseeded then cut into 2cm/¾in pieces

1 Heat the oil in a large saucepan over low heat. Lightly fry the onion and garlic together. Add the aubergine and pepper; lightly fry.

800g/1¾lb vine or plum tomatoes, cut into quarters
3 teaspoons tomato purée
1 teaspoon ground coriander
12 chestnut mushrooms, cut into quarters
Salt and freshly ground black pepper
A little butter
225g/8oz Merguez or any other spicy sausages
3 courgettes, cut in half and then into 2cm/¾in slices

2 Add the tomatoes, tomato purée, ground coriander and mushrooms. Season, stir well and cook over a gentle heat with the lid on for 20–30 minutes until the aubergine is soft. Meanwhile, in a frying pan, fry the sausages gently in a little butter for 15–20 minutes, turning occasionally. Add the courgettes to the ratatouille 10 minutes before the end of the cooking time.

To Serve:
Couscous (page 110)

3 To serve, check the seasoning, then pile the ratatouille on plates. Cut the sausages in half and place on top. Try with couscous.

FILLET STEAK WITH SPICY SALSA

Although this steak is marinaded overnight, the salsa is very quick and easy to whip up. For a variation, thinly slice the steak when cooked, pile high the slices and top with salsa and sour cream.

Utensils Plastic or china container (for marinading), large heatproof bowl, mixing bowl and large frying pan

2 x 175g/6oz fillet steaks preferably Aberdeen Angus
4 tablespoons olive oil
1 lemon, zested and juiced

1 Marinade the steak by mixing the oil, lemon zest and juice in a plastic or china container big enough to take the meat. Turn the steaks over in the mixture a few times, cover and leave overnight.

3 medium vine or plum tomatoes

2 To make the salsa, put the tomatoes in a heatproof bowl and cover with boiling water. Leave for 1 minute. Check that the skin will easily peel away, then plunge into very cold water. Cut in half horizontally and remove the seeds with a teaspoon, then cut into 1cm/½in squares.

½ medium red onion
1 red chilli

3 Chop the onion finely. Deseed the chilli by cutting it in half lengthways and scraping the seeds out with a teaspoon. Chop finely.

15g/¾oz fresh mint
15g/¾oz fresh coriander
1 lime, zested and juiced
3 tablespoons olive oil
Salt and freshly ground black pepper

4 Roughly chop the mint and coriander. In a bowl, mix together the prepared salsa ingredients. Add the lime zest, juice, oil and seasoning. Cover and refrigerate until needed. If serving potatoes of any kind, start to prepare them now before cooking the steak.

Freshly ground black pepper

5 Place a frying pan over a high heat and when hot, scrape away any excess oil from the steaks and put them in the pan. Season with freshly ground black pepper and cook for 4 minutes on either side for a medium-rare steak. Adjust the timing according to your preference.

To Serve:
Chilli oil, a little sour cream, and Oven Roasted Chips (page 94)

6 Put each steak on a warm plate, then pile high with salsa, drizzle with chilli oil and spoon a little sour cream on top. Serve with Oven Roasted Chips.

HERB-CRUSTED SALMON WITH SAUCE VIERGE

Utensils Food processor, small frying pan, small baking tray, large heatproof bowl and small saucepan

Herb Crust:
100g/3½oz white bread
½ small garlic clove
2 sprigs fresh rosemary or thyme
2 tablespoons chopped flat leaf parsley
1 tablespoon olive oil
Salt and freshly ground black pepper

1 Place the bread in the bowl of the food processor and pulse for a few seconds to make fine breadcrumbs. Add the garlic and herbs, pulse again and pour into a bowl. Stir in the oil; season.

Salt and freshly ground black pepper
2 x 175–200g/6–7oz slices of salmon fillet (organic or wild), skinned
Small knob of butter

2 Season the fish and heat the butter in a small frying pan. When foaming, add the seasoned fish and fry for a few seconds on both sides. Remove the fish from the pan, divide the breadcrumb mixture in two and press firmly onto each fillet. Place both fillets on a small baking tray. They can be kept, covered, in the fridge or a short while until you are ready.

4 vine or plum tomatoes

3 Skin the tomatoes by placing them in a heatproof bowl. Pour boiling water on top and leave for 1 minute. Check the skins can be removed, plunge into cold water, then peel off the skins. Cut in half, remove the seeds with a teaspoon and cut into ½cm/¼in squares. If serving potatoes, cook them now. Turn on the grill to its highest setting and preheat the oven to 200°C/400°F/Gas 6.

4 teaspoons lemon juice
55ml/2 fl oz olive oil
2 tablespoons water
5 basil leaves, shredded
Pinch of sugar

4 Put the lemon juice, olive oil, water, salt and pepper and basil in a small saucepan with the sugar and heat through gently.

5 Place the salmon underneath the grill for 2 minutes until golden brown, then finish off in the oven for 4-6 minutes. Add the tomatoes to the dressing to gently heat through; they should not overcook.

To Serve:
New potatoes and chopped chives

6 Place the fillets carefully on plates and spoon a little dressing on the side. Serve with new potatoes and garnish with plenty of chopped chives.

SALMON WRAPPED IN FILO PASTRY WITH GINGER AND SULTANAS

Serves 2
Preparation and Cooking Time:
40 minutes

This is an old recipe which has been updated using filo pastry, which can now be found, either frozen or fresh, in most supermarkets. The pastry is quite fiddly to use at first but with a little practice, you will be wrapping anything! The key is to keep it covered at all times with a damp cloth or tea towel. When wrapping, use it quite speedily and cover well with melted butter as it dries out very quickly. Ginger and sultanas complement the sweetness of the salmon.

Utensils Mixing bowl, small saucepan, pastry brush and small baking tray

10g/½oz piece preserved stem ginger, plus 2 teaspoons syrup reserved from jar
30g /1¼oz sultanas
1 lemon, zested and juiced
Salt and freshly ground black pepper

1 Thinly slice the ginger and then cut it into thin strips. Mix with the sultanas, lemon zest, juice and ginger syrup. Season.

¼ x 200g/7oz box filo pastry
50g/2oz butter

2 Open the filo pastry packet carefully and lay the layers flat on a work surface, keeping the pastry covered with a damp cloth or tea towel. In a small saucepan over low heat, melt the butter.

2 x 150g/5oz wild or organic salmon fillets, skinned

3 Season the salmon. Take one pastry sheet and use a sharp knife to cut it in half (each half should measure approximately 13 x 13cm/5 x 5in). Brush with plenty of melted butter and lay another sheet on top. Continue to layer, using a total of 4 sheets. Place half the ginger mixture evenly in the middle of each pastry square and place the salmon on top. Fold two sides together and press firmly to seal, then fold and seal the other ends.

4 Place the salmon parcels, join-side downwards, on the baking tray; brush with melted butter. (At this stage the parcels will hold for a couple of hours.)

To Serve:
New potatoes and a green salad

5 Preheat the oven to 190°C/375°F/Gas 5 and bake the salmon for 10–12 minutes. Serve with new potatoes and salad.

JAY KAY'S CREAMY POACHED COD WITH SPICY MASH

Serves 2

Preparation and Cooking Time:
25 minutes

Singer Jay Kay of Jamiroquai provided us with this deliciously creamy recipe for poached cod. Cod is widely available at all supermarkets nowadays and is at its best from September through February.

Utensils Ovenproof dish, medium saucepan and potato masher

1   Preheat the oven to 180°C/350°F/Gas 4.

2 cod fillets (175g/6oz each)
225ml/½ pint full fat milk
15g/¾oz butter
Salt and freshly ground black pepper

2   Put the cod in an ovenproof dish, cover with milk and butter. Season well and cover the dish with foil. Bake for 20 minutes or until cooked.

2 large potatoes

3   Meanwhile, peel and halve the potatoes and put them in a saucepan of cold, salted water. Bring to the boil over a medium heat and simmer for 20–25 minutes.

½ red chilli, deseeded
Sprig of parsley
½ red onion

4   Chop the chilli, parsley and red onion finely as you'll be adding these to the mashed potato.

A knob of butter

5   When the potatoes are ready (they should be soft; test them with a sharp knife), mash them well, adding the butter and seasoning. When any lumps have gone, add the chilli, most of the parsley (reserve some for garnishing) and red onion.

To Serve:
Honey-glazed carrots, steamed asparagus and broccoli

6   To serve, place the mashed potato on warmed plates, making a bed for the fish; place the fish on top. Pour over some of the creamy sauce and sprinkle with parsley. If you want to serve this with vegetables, Jay suggests you try honey glazed carrots, steamed asparagus and broccoli.

SALMON PATE

This is an unbelievably easy and quick pâté using tinned red salmon and readily available prepackaged dairy products. The result is delicious.

Utensils Food processor

210g/7½oz tin red salmon, drained
200g/7oz soft cheese with garlic and herbs
½ medium lemon, juiced
1 heaped dessertspoon crème fraîche
1 heaped dessertspoon cream cheese
Salt and freshly ground black pepper
A few sprigs of fresh dill or tarragon (optional)

1 Place all the ingredients apart from the herbs together in a food processor and blend until smooth. If you're using herbs, add them to the bowl and blend again.

To Serve:
Crusty French bread or toasted flavoured bread, such as Caraway or Onion

2 Serve with crusty French or toasted flavoured bread.

PASTA PENNE WITH HERB COURGETTES AND PEPPER SALAD

Serves 2

Preparation and Cooking Time:
30–35 minutes

The key to this recipe is the delicious fresh herbs. Thanks to the cardamom, the salad has a unique flavour and it can be served on the side. This is a vegan dish but even ardent meat-eaters would be happy with it.

Utensils Baking tray, large saucepan with lid, pestle and mortar (optional), mixing bowl and large frying pan

1 Turn the grill on to its highest setting.

4 red peppers, halved, deseeded and stalks removed

2 Grill the peppers on a baking tray, skin side up, until the skins blacken. While hot, put them in a plastic bag or a saucepan with lid and leave to cool. The skin will then peel away easily. Slice lengthways into thin strips.

4 cardamom pods
1 tablespoon olive oil plus extra for frying and serving
1 teaspoon balsamic vinegar

3 Using the back of a spoon, crush the cardamom pods and remove the black seeds. Crush the seeds with the back of the spoon or in a pestle and mortar. Place in a bowl and stir in the peppers with the olive oil and balsamic vinegar. The mixture will keep overnight, covered, in the fridge.

About 4 tablespoons fresh herbs – try tarragon, chervil, parsley, dill and oregano, chopped (you can use all the herbs together or a combination)
250g/9oz penne pasta
450g/1lb medium courgettes

4 Boil a large saucepan of salted water for the penne. Chop the herbs. When the water is boiling, add the pasta and simmer for 8–10 minutes. Slice the courgettes and heat the olive oil in a large frying pan over a medium heat. Fry the courgettes without turning them so that they are lightly brown and quite crispy.

Salt and freshly ground black pepper

5 Drain the pasta. Add a little olive oil to the saucepan, add the pasta, season and mix well. Add the herbs to the courgettes and season.

6 Serve the courgettes piled on top of the pasta and serve the salad separately.

chapter five

the morning after – brunch

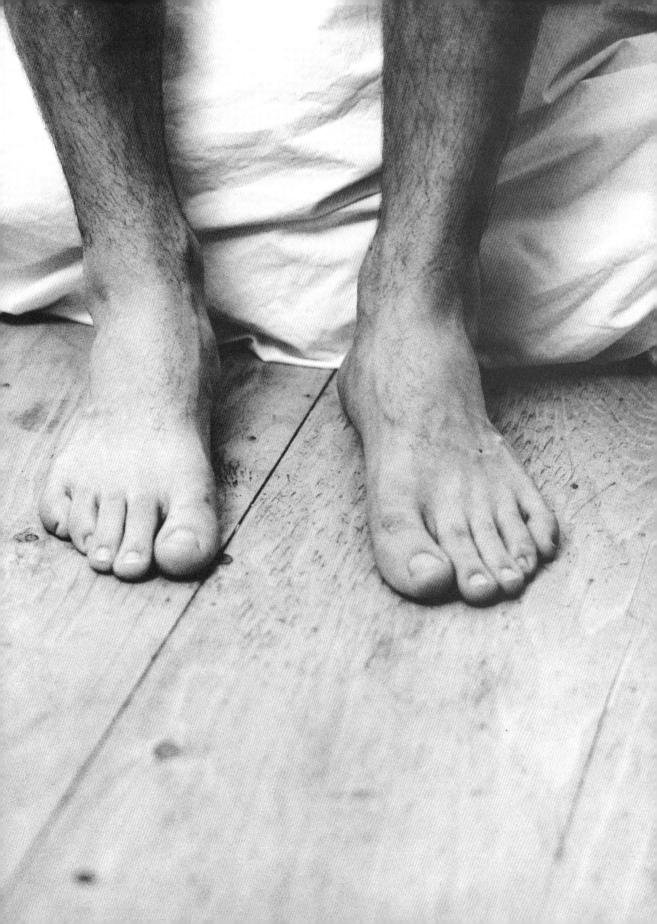

Ode to Your Sweetheart

Under the duvet, there's two pairs of feet,
One pair all hairy, the other quite neat.
The girl of your dreams is lying right there,
Body from *Baywatch* and long, curly hair.

It's taken you months and most of your pay,
To wine her and dine her and get her to stay.
Seeing her there your heart wants to sing,
For this is the one and not just a fling.

She opens her eyes and flashes that smile,
How can you make her stay for a while?
Too late for breakfast, too early for lunch,
Close your eyes sweetheart, I'll make you some brunch.

CINNAMON FRENCH TOAST

This delicious brunch dish is very popular in the USA. In New York City in particular they often substitute regular white bread with Challah bread – an enriched sweet variety which is cut into thick slices, making their French Toast generally far superior. It is crispy on the outside and moist and gooey on the inside. Another variation is to use a croissant split in half lengthways – delicious.

Utensils Shallow mixing bowl, large non-stick frying pan, palette knife and small bowl

2 medium eggs
2 thick slices of white bread, cut from a fresh loaf

1 Break the eggs into a shallow bowl and whisk with a fork. Cut the slices of bread on the diagonal to make triangles and press them into the egg mixture.

Knob of butter

2 Melt the butter in a large frying pan over a low heat and when foaming, add the egg-soaked bread. After a couple of minutes, use a palette knife to turn the bread over – the underside should be golden brown. Repeat until both sides are golden.

4 teaspoons caster sugar
1 teaspoon ground cinnamon

3 While the bread is cooking, mix together the sugar and cinnamon in a small bowl.

4 Onto warmed plates, arrange the two bread triangles and sprinkle with the cinnamon sugar. Serve immediately. French Toast can also be served with sliced bananas and maple syrup – enough to satisfy anyone's sweet tooth!

EASY PANCAKES
WITH MAPLE SYRUP

Real maple syrup should be used rather than a syrup with a maple flavouring as nothing comes close to the real thing.

Utensils Food processor, large bowl, large non-stick frying pan and whisk

½ teacup milk
1 medium egg
1 medium egg yolk

1 Using a food processor, mix the milk, whole egg and egg yolk together (saving the one white to add to the three more whites you'll use later in the recipe).

1 teacup plain flour
½ teaspoon baking powder
½ teaspoon bicarbonate of soda
Pinch of salt

2 Add the flour, baking powder and bicarbonate of soda to the batter mixture. Blend again, add seasoning and pour into a large bowl.

4 egg whites

3 Whisk the egg whites until firm, stir a quarter of them into the mixture, then carefully fold in the rest.

A little sunflower oil for frying

4 Heat a non-stick frying pan with a little sunflower oil over a medium heat. When the oil is hot, spoon a tablespoon of the pancake mixture into the pan and leave for 2–3 minutes or until the top looks semi-firm and the underside is brown. Use a large metal spatula to flip the pancake over and fry for a few seconds on the other side. The mixture should make approximately 8 pancakes. Wrap in foil and keep warm in a low oven (140°C/275°F/Gas 1).

To serve:
Maple syrup

5 Pile 4 warm pancakes onto each hot plate and drizzle with maple syrup.

Top Man Tip For a summer variation, warm a punnet of blueberries in a saucepan with a little water and sugar over a low heat. The berries are ready when the juices are released. Serve warm with the pancakes.

PINK GRAPEFRUIT AND ORANGE SALAD

Serves 2
Preparation Time: 15 minutes

Most women watching their waistlines would thank you for this refreshing and light breakfast dish. You could also add fresh dates if you wish.

Utensils Serrated knife and medium bowl

2 medium oranges
1 pink grapefruit

1 Cut the ends away from the oranges and grapefruit and place them, cut side down, on a chopping board. Using a serrated knife, follow the curved line of the fruit and slice away the peel, making sure all the white pith is removed.

2 Holding the fruit over a bowl, cut each segment away from the encasing pith. Mix in a separate bowl and chill, covered, until needed.

1 bunch fresh mint, to garnish

3 To serve, pile into 2 chilled long glasses and garnish with mint sprigs.

SMOKED TROUT WITH SCRAMBLED EGGS

Serves 2
Preparation and Cooking Time:
10 minutes

Smoked trout is readily available in supermarkets. As an alternative to smoked salmon, it is cheaper and more than adequate for this kind of recipe. This is an old favourite and it is just as good as a supper dish as first thing in the morning.

Utensils Small saucepan and mixing bowl

140g/4¾oz sliced smoked trout or smoked salmon

1 Arrange the smoked trout or salmon on two plates.

A small knob of butter
8 free range eggs
Salt and freshly ground black pepper

2 Melt the butter in a small saucepan over a low heat. Whisk the eggs in a bowl, season and add to the saucepan. As in all egg dishes, they must be cooked very gently. Stirring continuously, cook for about 5 minutes or until the eggs are just coagulating but still quite runny. They will continue to cook when the heat is turned off.

1 lemon
Chopped chives

3 To serve, pile the eggs on top of the trout and season. Add a good squeeze of lemon juice and sprinkle with chopped chives. Serve straight away.

EGGS BENEDICT

This classic egg brunch dish may seem daunting and a little fiddly but once you've done it a couple of times, you will really appreciate making the effort. The combination of rich Hollandaise Sauce with delicately poached eggs and tasty bacon is insurpassable. Try to get good-quality, dry-cured bacon; it makes all the difference (page 159). Generally, prepackaged factory bacon has been cured using an instant method whereby chemicals are injected into the meat. This is the water seen seeping out during cooking.

Utensils Medium Pyrex or metal bowl (to fit over a large saucepan) large saucepan, whisk, timer, medium baking tray, and slotted spoon

110g/4oz butter, straight from the fridge

1 Start by making the Hollandaise Sauce, which will hold for a while while you prepare the rest of the ingredients. Take a Pyrex or metal bowl which will fit over a saucepan without touching the bottom. Cut the very cold and hard butter into 2cm/¾in cubes.

2 medium free range eggs

2 Quarter-fill the saucepan with water; the bowl should not be touching the water. Bring to simmering point. Separate the 2 egg yolks from the whites and whisk the yolks into the bowl over the heat while the water is beginning to simmer. After a few seconds, add a couple of cubes of butter and whisk again. As the butter melts into the yolks, slowly add the remaining butter, a couple of cubes at a time, whisking continuously. Gradually the eggs and butter will emulsify and create a thick but light sauce. Whisk until a good consistency has been reached.

Juice of ½ medium lemon
Salt and freshly ground black pepper

3 Remove the bowl from the saucepan, stir in the lemon juice and season. Cover with clingfilm and keep somewhere warm.

4 Turn the grill to its highest setting and put the plates to warm in a low oven (140°C/275°F/Gas 1).

4 medium free range eggs for poaching

5 Now for poaching the eggs. Using the same saucepan, turn down the heat and when the water is barely simmering, crack each egg into the pan. Poach for 2 minutes: use a timer if you have one. When the time is up, turn off the heat and leave the eggs in the saucepan for a further 5 minutes.

4 slices back bacon
2 English muffins

6 Grill the bacon and halved muffin on a baking tray (the muffin only needs to be toasted for 1 minute), then put on the hot plates.

7 Turn the bacon over and grill for about ½ minute. Check the temperature of the Hollandaise Sauce. If it needs to be rewarmed, put the bowl back over the saucepan of hot water and whisk again.

To serve:
Salt and freshly ground black pepper

8 Put the bacon on top of the muffin halves. Use a slotted spoon to remove the poached eggs from the saucepan. Drain on kitchen paper or a tea towel, then place the eggs on top of the bacon. Season, cover with Hollandaise Sauce and serve immediately. If necessary, flash under the grill to warm through.

Top Man Tip Eggs for poaching must be totally fresh. Another variation on this brunch dish is to substitute smoked salmon garnished with chopped chives for the bacon.

SMOKED SALMON AND CREAM CHEESE BAGELS

Serves 2
Preparation Time: 5 minutes

Always a winner! Although the bagels in this country seem a little doughy and heavy, when toasted they gain a slightly better texture.

Utensils Mixing bowl

15g/¾oz fresh chives
200g/7oz cream cheese
Freshly ground black pepper

1 Chop the chives finely and mix them in a bowl with the cream cheese. Season with black pepper.

2 bagels, fresh from the bakery (better and lighter than packaged)

2 Split the bagels in two and toast lightly. Spread the cream cheese generously over each warmed half.

70g/2¾oz smoked salmon
Juice of 1 lemon or lime

3 Top with a pile of smoked salmon, a good squeeze of lemon or lime juice and black pepper.

who needs mother?

Church bells, huge piles of newspapers and lunch-

time beers in the pub can only mean one day – Sunday. And what

could be more quintessential to Sundays than a roast lunch?

It isn't as hard as you may think; it just takes a little preparation

and planning – hopefully our timing chart will help you get

organised. When shopping for your roast it's always worth

spending a little extra to buy good-quality, preferably free-range

meat from a reputable butcher.

The Roasting Plan

We thought it would be an idea to show you what roasts we've
covered in this chapter and the accompaniments that we suggest you
put with them. We've also included approximate timings for cooking
each roasted meat per kg/lb. We discuss these in more detail in each
individual recipe. Amounts are given assuming that you will be cooking
for six people.

The time plan is for a 1 o'clock lunch. This gives you a good outline of
how to plan your preparation, but adjust the timings to suit what time
you want to eat. As with all our recipes, these timings are based on
using a fan oven. For all other ovens, follow the manufacturer's
recommendations carefully (see page 5).

Roasting Chart

Pork (page 66)	Marinaded Roast/Grilled Lamb (page 69)	Lemon Roast Chicken (page 68)	Roast Beef (page 70)
2.25kg/5lb Loin of pork. Bone removed and rolled.	2.25kg/5lb Leg of lamb, boned. Marinaded overnight.	2 x 1.8kg/4lb chicken	2.25kg/5lb rib joint/wing end.
15 minutes per 450g (lb) + 15 minutes	5 minutes per 450g (lb) or grilled 20 minutes each side	10 minutes per 450g (lb)	15 minutes per 450g (lb) + 5 minutes
Oven 220°C/ 425°F/Gas 7 then 190°C/375°F/Gas 5	Oven 200°C/400°F/Gas 6	Oven 200°C/400°F/Gas 6 then 190°C/375°F/Gas 5	Oven 200°C/400°F/Gas 6 then 190°C/375°F/Gas 5
In oven by 11:30 a.m.	In oven by 12:25 p.m. or grill at 12:20 p.m.	In oven by 12:05 p.m.	In oven by 11:30 a.m.
Take out of oven at 12:45 pm.	Take out of oven at 12:50 p.m.	Take out of oven at 12:45 p.m.	Take out of oven at 12:50 p.m.
Rest 15 minutes	Rest 10 minutes	Rest 10–15 minutes	Rest 10 minutes
Roast Potatoes (page 67) As the temperature will be higher, they will not take so long to cook.	**Potato Gratin or Boulangère Potatoes** (page 113)	**Roast Potatoes** (page 67)	**Roast Potatoes** (page 67)
11:30 a.m. Start to prepare and par boil potatoes.	11:50 a.m. Start to prepare and par boil.	11.30 a.m. Start to prepare and par boil.	11.30 a.m. Start to prepare and par boil.
In oven by 12:10 p.m. Cook for 20–25 minutes. Take out at 12:35 p.m. and reheat for 5 minutes.	In the bottom of the oven by 12 p.m. Cook for 1 hour.	In the oven by 12:10 p.m. When the meat is resting, the heat can be turned up to finish.	In the oven by 12:10 p.m. Take out 12:50 p.m; keep warm.
Braised Red Cabbage with Apple (page 109) 11:45 a.m. Start to prepare.	**Sautéed Mushrooms and Asparagus** (page 123) Blanch the asparagus and prepare the mushrooms.	**Cumin Beans** (page 116) 12:10 p.m. Prepare the beans, cumin, tomatoes and onions. 12:45 p.m. Put the pan of water on to boil. 12:55 p.m. Finish the beans.	**Peas with Rocket and Spring Onions** (page 115) 12.10 p.m. Cook and reheat.
Cook on hob as there will be limited space in the oven.	12:55 p.m. When the meat is resting and everything is finished off, stir fry the mushrooms and asparagus, then serve.	12: 50 p.m. Finish the gravy/jus.	**Yorkshire Pudding** (page 71) 11:30 a.m. Make batter and leave to rest. 12:50 p.m. When the meat is resting, turn the heat up for Yorkshire Pudding. Whisk the whites, mix and cook for 15–20 minutes.
Apple Compôte (page 66) 12:10 p.m. Prepare the apples. This can be cooked in the bottom of the oven.			
Gravy (page 67) 12:45 p.m. Make while the meat is resting.			**Gravy** (page 67). Make at 12:45 p.m. while the meat is resting.

ROAST PORK WITH APPLE COMPOTE

The loin of pork is the best cut to roast. It should be roasted quickly and not overcooked. The crackling protects it from drying out; ensure the surface has been well scored (preferably by your butcher) as the fennel mixture should be pushed well into the incisions. A layer of Maldon salt will help with the crackling process. Do not baste the meat and try to resist opening the oven door!

Utensils: Pestle and mortar, large, deep roasting tin and large ovenproof dish

1 Preheat the oven to 220°C/425°F/Gas 7.

2.25kg/5lb loin of pork (boned and rolled, skin on)
1½ garlic cloves
2 tablespoons fennel seeds
1 tablespoon Maldon salt
Freshly ground black pepper

2 Using a sharp knife, score the skin of the pork deeply over the whole surface, about 5mm/¼in apart. Using a pestle and mortar, crush the garlic cloves and fennel seeds, mix with the salt and pepper and push well into the incisions. Place in a roasting tin and roast, uncovered, for 1 hour 15 minutes (or 15 mins per 450g [lb]). After 15 minutes, turn the oven down to 190°C/375°F/Gas 5.

Apple Compôte:
5 apples
A little butter
Salt and freshly ground black pepper

3 While the pork is roasting, bake the Apple Compôte. Peel and core 5 apples, cut into quarters and slice thinly. Put a little butter into an ovenproof dish and fill with apple. Cover well with foil. Bake in the bottom of the oven for 30–40 minutes. When cooked, stir and season.

4 Remove the meat from the roasting tin and wrap in foil (remove the crackling first or it will become soggy). Leave to rest in a warm place for about 15 minutes.

Gravy (pages 65 and 67)

5 Make the gravy on the hob if there is room.

To Serve:
Apple Compôte, Roast Potatoes (pages 65 and 67) and Braised Red Cabbage with Apple (pages 65 and 109)

6 Carve the meat and serve with Gravy, Apple Compôte, Roast Potatoes and Braised Red Cabbage with Apple.

Gravy

Utensils Roasting tin, whisk, small sieve and small saucepan

3 tablespoons melted fat (left over from roasting the meat)
3 tablespoons plain flour

425ml/¾ pint vegetable stock made from granules (or vegetable water)
A few sprigs of fresh herbs such as rosemary, tarragon or sage, chopped
1 glass red wine
Gravy browning (optional)
Salt and freshly ground black pepper

1 Pour away any excess fat from the roasting tin used to roast the meat, leaving any sediment at the bottom. Place the tin over a medium heat, add the flour and stir well for a few seconds.

2 Stir in the prepared stock a little at a time, making sure it is absorbed into the liquid before adding more. A whisk may be better than a spoon for this stage. When the gravy gets to a thick sauce-like consistency, pour it through a sieve into a small pan to get rid of any remaining lumps. Add the herbs and the wine and simmer for 3–4 minutes to cook out the flour and wine. You can also add a little gravy browning if desired at this stage to give a darker colour. Taste and check your seasoning.

3 Serve the gravy piping hot. If you don't want to use the gravy straight away, leave it in the saucepan and reheat as and when required.

Roast Potatoes

Utensils Large saucepan, large colander and very large baking tray

1 Preheat the oven to 200°C/400°F/Gas 6.

1.8kg/4lb Potatoes (Maris Piper, Red Desiree, Whites)
Maldon salt

2 Peel and cut the potatoes to size (approximately 5cm/2in squares). Place them in a saucepan and cover with cold, salted water. Bring to the boil and simmer for 5 minutes.

A large knob of butter
3 tablespoons olive oil

3 Put the butter and oil in the baking tray and place in the oven so that they are well heated before you add the potatoes.

4 Meanwhile, drain the potatoes in a colander, shaking them well to form a rough-ish edge. This is the secret to a crunchy roast potato. Pour the potatoes carefully into the now-hot oil in the baking tray, return to the oven and roast for 20 minutes. Turn them over and cook for another 20 minutes.

5 To serve, line a warm serving dish with kitchen paper. Pour the potatoes into the dish, sprinkle with a good pinch of salt and pull away the paper just before serving.

LEMON ROAST CHICKEN

This adaptation of a Simon Hopkinson recipe is unlike any other roast chicken recipe. It's very simple and aside from the subtle flavour of lemon and garlic which perfectly enhances the chicken, it has the added bonus that its own delicious gravy or 'jus' is made during the roasting process. When roasting a chicken, it is better to spend that little bit extra on a superior bird. Try to go for corn-fed or free range.

Utensils Large roasting tin, a small saucepan and sieve

1 Preheat the oven to 200°C/400°F/Gas 6.

50g/2oz unsalted butter at room temperature
2 x 1.8kg/4lb free range chickens

2 Smear the butter over each chicken and place them uncovered and breast down in a large roasting tin.

Salt and freshly ground black pepper
2 lemons, halved and juiced
30g/1¼oz thyme or tarragon
2 cloves of garlic, peeled
275ml/½ pint vegetable stock

3 Season well, then place the squeezed-out lemon halves inside the bird's cavity, along with the herbs and garlic. Pour over the vegetable stock.

4 Place the chickens, uncovered, in the oven. After 10 minutes, baste the bird and turn the oven down to 190°C/375°F/Gas 5. Roast for 50 minutes.

5 Check that the chicken is cooked by cutting through the leg: no blood should run from the thigh. Take the chicken out of the oven, remove the lemon, herbs and garlic from the cavity and add them to the roasting tin to help flavour the gravy/jus. Let the cooked chicken rest in a warm place, covered in foil, for approximately 15 minutes.

1 teacup white wine

6 Add the wine and extra seasoning to the roasting tin, scraping the bottom of the pan as you stir over a medium heat. Push the lemons around the tin to extract all their remaining juices and leave to simmer gently for 5 minutes while the chicken is resting. Strain into a saucepan.

To Serve:
Roast Potatoes (page 67) and
Cumin Beans (page 116)

7 To serve, return the chicken to the roasting tin to carve it and pour any extra juices into the gravy saucepan. Reheat the gravy/jus and serve with Roast Potatoes and Cumin Beans.

MARINADED ROAST/ GRILLED LAMB

Lamb is good from February to March when it has developed a really full flavour. New season lamb is at its best in May and, coincidentally, this is the best time for asparagus. The combination of the two is unique. There are many recipes for roast lamb. We have included a method which doesn't need very long to cook on a griddle or in the oven. It's also great barbecued. Ask your butcher to do the boning for you – what you want is a large piece of even meat. Barts Spices make a smoked paprika which has an interesting flavour. If unobtainable, ordinary paprika will suffice.

Utensils Large shallow dish (for marinading the lamb) and a large griddle or roasting tin

Marinade:

1 cup walnut oil
1 large bunch fresh oregano
(about 30g/1¼oz)
20 crushed juniper berries
2 tablespoons smoked or
ordinary paprika

2.25kg/5lb leg of lamb, boned
Salt and freshly ground black
pepper

1   Mix all the ingredients for the marinade in a dish large enough to take the meat. Make sure the lamb is completely covered in the marinade's pungent oils and flavourings. Season the lamb and leave, covered, in the fridge for as long as you can (preferably overnight).

2   Heat a large griddle over a high heat, season the meat well and cook for 20 minutes on each side depending on how pink you like your meat. Alternatively, if you're using an oven, preheat it to 200°C/400°F/Gas 6. Place the meat directly on the oven rack, uncovered, with a roasting tin underneath (or Boulangère Potatoes, see page 122), or you can put it in a tin and roast for 30 minutes. As this is an unusual cut of meat, treat it as if you were roasting a large steak of meat.

To Serve:

Chopped fresh mint, Roast
Potatoes (page 67) and
Sautéed Mushrooms and
Asparagus (page 123)

3   Remove the lamb from the oven and leave it to rest, covered in foil, in a warm place for approximately 10 minutes. Carve carefully to reveal the succulent pink meat underneath the crisply charred caramelised skin. If cooked in the oven in a roasting tin there will be plenty of juices and these may be served as a clear gravy with chopped fresh mint added. Serve with Roast Potatoes and Sautéed Mushrooms and Asparagus.

Top Man Tip To bone the lamb yourself, find the place where the long bone runs down the length of the leg: it appears quite close to the surface. Using a sharp knife, open the meat along this bone. Cut the meat back on either side. At the wider end of the leg there are smaller bones. Cut round them and the whole bone will lift away to leave two large sections of meat. Cut into these and fold the meat over to level out. The whole piece should roughly be 5cm/2in thick.

ROAST BEEF

Traditional Roast Beef and Yorkshire Pudding needs no introduction. A classic English favourite, we believe it should be served pink to get the full benefit from this succulent cut of beef. Remember to take the beef out of the fridge one hour before cooking to adapt its temperature.

Utensils Roasting tin

1 Preheat the oven to 200°C/400°F/Gas 6.

2 tablespoons grainy mustard
2 tablespoons Dijon mustard
2.25kg/5lb boned and rolled rib joint (wing end or Sirloin of beef)
Maldon salt
Freshly ground black pepper

2 Mix the two mustards together, spread them over the fat around the meat and season well.

3 Put the meat in a roasting tin in the oven for 5 minutes, then turn the oven down to 190°C/375°F/Gas 5 for 1 hour 15 minutes, basting occasionally.

To Serve:
Gravy (page 67), Yorkshire Pudding (page 71) and Peas with Rocket and Spring Onions (page 115)

4 To serve, take the meat out of the oven and leave to rest, covered in foil, on top of the hob. Carve off thick slices and serve with Gravy, Yorkshire Pudding and Peas with Rocket and Spring Onions.

A little red wine
Fresh herbs such as tarragon and thyme

Top Man Tip For the best Roast Beef gravy, stir in a little red wine and some fresh herbs.

YORKSHIRE PUDDING

This recipe beats any other Yorkshire pudding. The lightly whipped egg whites that are folded in at the end create a truly light, fluffy version that simply melts in your mouth.

Utensils Food processor, non-stick muffin tin (to hold 12 puddings), mixing bowl and a hand whisk

2 eggs
110g/4oz plain flour
275ml/½ pint full fat milk
Salt and freshly ground black pepper

1 In a food processor, blend together the eggs, flour, milk and seasoning to a smooth liquid/batter. Leave to stand for 30 minutes.

2 Preheat the oven to 200°C/400°F/Gas 6.

Large knob of lard

3 Rub a little lard into each indentation of the muffin tin and place in the oven to heat through.

2 egg whites

4 In a bowl, whisk the egg whites together with a hand whisk until white and firm. After the batter has been left to rest, stir half the egg whites into the batter mixture and carefully fold in the rest.

5 Pour the batter into the hot muffin tin and place on a high shelf in the oven. Cook for 15–20 minutes until golden brown.

6 Serve directly from the oven in all their fluffy glory!

Top Man Tip If you're cooking the puddings to serve with meat, you can cook your Yorkshire while the meat is resting.

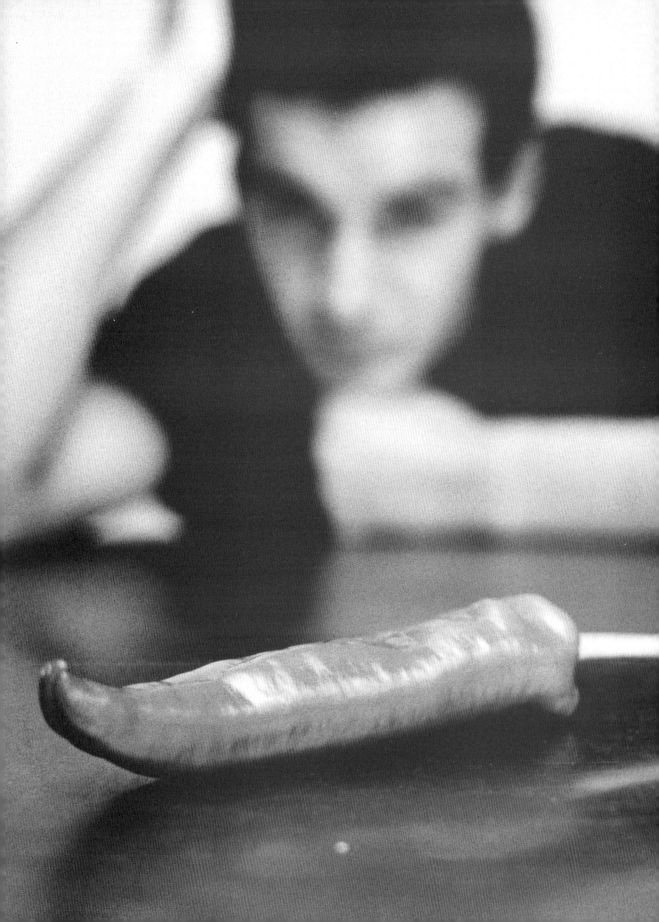

chapter seven

some
like
it hot

Spices were once considered 'foreign'

but are now an integral part of British cooking. Preparing spices yourself may take a little longer than using ready-made pastes but they taste so much better. Familiarising yourself with the many varieties now available is a learning process to be enjoyed and will enhance your cooking skills enormously. We have included details of an excellent mail order company (see page 159) to make it easier for you to obtain the more unusual spices.

Serves 4
Preparation and Cooking Time:
30–35 minutes

CHICKEN KORMA

With a little organisation on the spice front, this recipe is a far superior version of a well loved dish. It is quite rich, but suitable for a special occasion and your efforts will be much appreciated.

Utensils Coffee grinder or pestle and mortar, large saucepan or frying pan or ovenproof casserole

½ teaspoon cumin seeds (or preground)
½ teaspoon mustard seeds (or preground)
½ teaspoon fenugreek (or preground)
½ teaspoon coriander seeds (or preground)

1 If using whole spices, in a coffee grinder or pestle and mortar, grind the cumin, mustard, fenugreek and coriander seeds together.

1 teaspoon cardamom pods
½ teaspoon cayenne
2 pinches cinnamon
2 pinches allspice
2 pinches ground nutmeg

2 Crush the cardamom pods with the back of a spoon or in a pestle and mortar to release their black seeds. Add the seeds, together with the cayenne, cinnamon, allspice and nutmeg to the already ground spice mixture and blend again as before.

900g/2lb chicken breasts
2 cloves garlic
I medium onion
4cm/1½in piece fresh ginger, peeled

3 Cut the chicken into bite-size pieces. Crush the garlic, chop the onion and grate the ginger.

2 tablespoons vegetable oil
Salt and freshly ground black pepper

4 Heat the vegetable oil in a large saucepan or frying pan or ovenproof casserole over a medium heat. Lightly fry the chicken pieces, season and add the onion, garlic and ginger. After 3–4 minutes, add the prepared spices and cook for a couple of minutes to release their flavours.

5 If you're serving this dish with Basmati Rice, begin cooking it now.

250ml/8 fl oz chicken stock
275ml/½ pint whipping cream
90g/3oz creamed coconut from a 200g/7oz block

6 Add the stock, cream and creamed coconut to the spicy chicken and simmer for 15 minutes. The sauce will reduce to the consistency of thick cream.

To Serve:
Basmati Rice (page 120)
15g/¾oz chopped fresh coriander, to garnish

5 Check the seasoning and serve with Basmati Rice with chopped fresh coriander sprinkled on top or forked through the rice.

Top Man Tip The best way to peel ginger is either with a very sharp knife or a potato peeler. Always look for large, firm pieces of ginger; avoid anything that appears to be dried and too old.

CHICKEN TAGINE

These spices are unusual and sometimes difficult to find, but they can be purchased by mail order (page 159), which takes the hassle out of hunting around. It is worth investing in a good collection of spices as they keep well in your store cupboard. All you then have to do is add a couple of fresh ingredients to achieve this simple, but undeniably luxurious dish. By the way, Ras El Hanout is: cubebs, rose petals, fennel, grains of paradise, dill seeds, mace, cumin, cassia, chillies, nutmeg, turmeric, pepper, cloves, cardamoms, liquorice and ginger!

Utensils Large, shallow ovenproof or earthenware lidded dish

1 Preheat the oven to 190°C/375°F/Gas 5.

900g/2lb potatoes, Red Desiree if possible
3 cloves garlic
15g/¾oz fresh coriander
2 large onions

2 Peel and very thinly slice the potatoes. Finely chop the garlic, coriander and onions.

A little olive oil
4 whole chicken legs, skinned and cut in two
Salt and plenty of freshly ground black pepper
1 teaspoon ground ginger
½ teaspoon Ras El Hanout
2 large pinches saffron
½ teaspoon ground cinnamon

3 Pour a little olive oil into a large ovenproof or earthenware dish, place it over a medium heat and add the chicken. Season and sprinkle the spices over the chicken. Gently fry for 3 minutes.

200g/7oz green olives

4 Sprinkle the chopped garlic, coriander, onions and olives over the chicken, season and top with a layer of potato.

½ teacup cold water

5 Add the water, cover and bake in the oven for 45 minutes to 1 hour or until the potatoes are cooked.

To Serve:
Spiced Aubergine Salad
(page 130)

6 Serve with Spiced Aubergine Salad and caraway bread if available.

LAMB WITH SMOKED PAPRIKA AND BUTTERNUT SQUASH

Serves 4
Preparation and Cooking Time:
1 hour 45 minutes

Butternut squash is available all year round and is a great vegetable to roast, as well as to add to a dish such as this as it keeps its shape. Smoked paprika gives an unusual and delicate smoked twist to anything. It is widely available as a Barts Spice and is now sold in most supermarkets. If you don't come across it though, ordinary paprika will suffice.

Utensils Large casserole dish with lid

1kg/2¼lb lamb (leg or shoulder)
A little vegetable or sunflower oil
Salt and freshly ground black pepper

1 Cut the meat into 4cm/1½in squares. Heat the oil in a casserole dish over medium high heat, season the meat and fry a little at a time to seal; don't add too much at any one time as the meat will steam and won't brown.

1 medium onion
1 clove garlic
400g/14oz tin chopped tomatoes
2 teacups white wine
2 teaspoons smoked paprika
3 teacups vegetable stock
2 sprigs fresh oregano or thyme, picked into small pieces

2 Preheat the oven to 150°C/300°F/Gas 2. Chop the onion and garlic finely and cook with the last batch of meat. Add the tomatoes, wine, paprika, stock and herbs. Season and bring to a simmer, along with all the browned meat. Replace the lid and cook in the oven for 1 hour.

1 medium size butternut squash

3 Peel the squash with a sharp knife or potato peeler, remove the seeds and cut into 4cm/1½in squares. After the hour is up, stir the squash into the meat and cook for a further ½ hour.

To Serve:
Saffron Mash (page 106)

4 This recipe can be cooked in advance and then reheated. Save the squash and add it at the end when you reheat this dish for ½ hour. It is particularly good served with Saffron Mash.

Top Man Tip It is worth allowing the time to cut your own meat or getting your butcher to do it for you, as precut, packaged stuff is normally far too small and uneven.

LENNOX LEWIS'S JAMAICAN JERK CHICKEN WITH RICE

Serves 4

Preparation and Cooking Time:
20 minutes

This dish was given to us by Lennox Lewis. Plantains can be found in African or Caribbean food stores and are typically used as a source of starch. For this recipe, try and find semi-ripe plantains, which are yellow and firm.

Utensils Medium saucepan, large saucepan for deep frying, slotted spoon, shallow bowl and a wok

275g/10oz long grain rice

1 Put the rice into a medium saucepan of boiling, salted water and simmer for 10 minutes with the lid on.

2 plantains
Vegetable oil for frying

2 Meanwhile, peel and thinly slice the plantains on the diagonal. Pour the vegetable oil into a deep saucepan and place over a medium heat. When the oil is hot, add the plantains and cook for 3 minutes or until golden brown. Take out with a slotted spoon and drain on kitchen paper. Leave to one side until needed.

4 chicken breasts, skinned and boned
4 teaspoons Jamaican Jerk seasoning
Salt and freshly ground black pepper

3 Cut the chicken into thin strips. Toss the strips in a bowl with the Jerk seasoning until they are well covered. Season with salt and freshly ground pepper.

4 Heat a little vegetable oil in a wok over a medium heat and stir fry the chicken for 3–4 minutes until firm.

5 To serve, drain the rice and serve with the hot chicken on top and plantains on the side.

Serves 4
Preparation and Cooking Time:
20 minutes and marinade
overnight, if possible

CHICKEN TIKKA

Using only a few spices for the marinade, a fresh and light version of this ever-popular Indian dish can be created. You can make the tandoori paste yourself if you like, but for convenience we have used a ready-made one which is just as good.

Utensils Mixing bowl, 4 metal or wooden skewers and a small baking tray

Marinade:
1 teaspoon fresh ginger, grated
1 teaspoon chopped garlic
½ teaspoon coriander seeds
½ teaspoon cumin seeds
1 teaspoon chilli powder
2 red chillies, finely chopped
1 teaspoon Garam Masala
3 tablespoons natural yoghurt
2 tablespoons lemon juice
2 tablespoons tandoori paste

900g/2lb chicken breasts, boned and skinned
Salt and freshly ground black pepper

1 In a bowl, mix together all the ingredients for the marinade.

2 Cut the chicken into small bite-size pieces, season and mix with the marinade. Cover and leave for as long as you can, preferably overnight in the fridge.

3 Spear the chicken pieces onto 4 metal or wooden skewers and place on a baking tray. Prepare any other accompaniments at this stage and then turn the grill to its highest setting.

4 Grill the chicken for 10–15 minutes, turning halfway through. Check carefully that the meat is cooked: it should be firm and white in colour.

To Serve:
Basmati Rice (page 120), mango chutney and Cucumber Raita (page 39)

5 Season as necessary and serve with Basmati Rice, mango chutney and Cucumber Raita.

Top Man Tip Do not use a metal container to marinade the meat, otherwise you'll end up with metal-tasting chicken!

chapter eight

you've cracked it!

Dinner parties nowadays aren't all about

smoking jackets, passing the mints and striving to impress with complex culinary masterpieces. You can afford to take it easy and think more informally.

Choose the right, well-rehearsed menu, plan ahead and do most of the preparation in advance and you won't end up losing your cool. Even shopping for your ingredients should be stress-free as supermarkets now provide pretty much everything you will need.

WATERCRESS SOUP

Although the quantity of watercress used in this recipe may seem excessive, it soon wilts down when cooked. Make sure it is thoroughly washed before you use it and remove any overly large, thick stems. When buying watercress, look for bright green, fresh-looking, large flat leaves. Bear in mind that during the summer months, watercress is not at its best.

Utensils Small and medium saucepans, and hand blender or food processor

1 medium onion
Knob of butter

1 Chop the onion. Melt the butter in a saucepan and over a medium heat, gently fry the onion until soft.

200g/7oz watercress, washed thoroughly
2 tablespoons plain flour
1 litre/1¾ pints vegetable or chicken stock
Salt and freshly ground black pepper

2 Add the watercress. When wilted, stir in the flour for a minute or so. Add the stock, season well and simmer, uncovered, for 20 minutes.

150ml/¼ pint whipping cream

3 Using a hand blender or food processor, blend the soup until it is totally smooth. Reheat gently as required, then add the whipping cream and reseason.

Beetroot Relish (optional):
Thin beetroot strips cut from 2 whole, cooked medium beets
A few capers
A little red onion
Splash of balsamic vinegar and olive oil

4 To make the relish, in a pan briefly cook thin strips of beetroot with a few capers, a little red onion and a splash each of balsamic vinegar and olive oil. Serve each bowl of soup topped with crème fraîche or Beetroot Relish.

To Serve:
Crème fraîche or Beetroot Relish

SWEETCORN CHOWDER

This is more of a light lunch soup. It's a classic recipe which again benefits from good, fresh ingredients. If you use fresh corn, scraped off the cob, and baby new potatoes, it will taste even better.

Utensils Medium saucepan and hand blender or food processor

1 medium onion
Knob of butter
2 x approximately 300g/11oz tins sweetcorn, drained
1 litre/1¾ pints vegetable stock
Salt and black pepper

1 Chop the onion, then melt the butter in a saucepan over a low heat and gently fry the onion for a few minutes until soft. Add the first tin of sweetcorn and the stock, season well and simmer, uncovered, for 20 minutes.

3 medium potatoes, approximately 450g/1lb
1 bunch (15g/¾oz) flat leaf parsley

2 While the soup is cooking, peel and chop the potatoes into small 1cm/½in cubes. (If using new potatoes, leave unpeeled.) Chop the parsley.

2 teacups full fat milk

3 Blend the cooked soup with a hand blender (you can do this in the saucepan) or in a food processor until it is very smooth. Put the soup back in the pan, add the raw potato, the second tin of sweetcorn and the milk. Simmer for a further 15–20 minutes or until the potato is cooked.

To Serve:
Crusty bread

4 Stir in the chopped parsley, check the seasoning and serve before the potato becomes too cooked and mushy. Serve with crusty bread.

FRENCH ONION SOUP

Contrary to popular belief, you don't need beef stock that has taken days to make to get a good onion soup. Even though the stock gives it a unique flavour, it is not essential. If the onions are caramelised and cooked well, their flavour will be enough to create a strong coloured, tasty traditional soup.

Utensils Food processor (if available), large saucepan, grater and small baking tray

4 large onions
1 large knob of butter

1 First slice the onions thinly. If you have a food processor, use the slicing blade for this as it will only take a few seconds. Melt the butter gently

Salt and freshly ground black pepper

in a large saucepan over a medium heat and add the onions to soften and caramelise. This adds flavour and colour. Season and cook, stirring occasionally, for 15 minutes or until golden brown.

275ml/½ pint red wine
1.5 litres/2½ pints vegetable stock
4 sprigs thyme, chopped

2 Add the red wine, reduce for a couple of minutes, then add the stock and thyme. Bring to the boil, then turn down the heat to just simmering for 45 minutes to 1 hour (it needs this length of time for the flavours to mature); season.

To Serve:
1 small baguette
75g/3oz Gruyère cheese, grated

3 Just before serving, turn the grill up to its highest setting. Cut the baguette into 4 x 2½cm/1in slices and pile high with grated cheese. Place on a small baking tray and grill until the cheese is melted and light brown.

4 Check the seasoning then serve the soup into warm bowls with a cheese croûte floating on top of each.

Serves 4
Preparation and Cooking Time:
35 minutes

LEEK AND POTATO SOUP

Always a winner! Even though this recipe may sound a little 70s, the soup really is a favourite and simply refuses to be swept under the carpet. The essential thing to remember is to use good-quality, fresh vegetables. Bear in mind that leeks are at their best in April.

Utensils Medium saucepan and hand blender or food processor

700g/1½lb potatoes
900g/2lb leeks
4 sprigs of thyme

1 Peel the potatoes and dice them into small cubes. Cut the leeks into1cm/½in slices and wash thoroughly. Remove the thyme leaves from their stems and chop roughly.

Knob of butter
Salt and freshly ground black pepper

2 Melt the butter in the saucepan, add the leeks, season and cook gently for a few minutes over a low heat.

1.5 litres/2½ pints vegetable or chicken stock

3 When the leeks start to soften, add the potatoes, thyme and stock. Simmer for 25 minutes over a medium heat.

4 Blend with a hand blender or food processor. Season and reheat as necessary.

To Serve:
1 small tub crème fraîche
15g/¾oz fresh chives, chopped

5 Onto each bowl of hot soup, float a heaped teaspoon of crème fraîche topped with lots of chopped chives.

CHICKEN SATAY WITH CUCUMBER SALAD

This classic South East Asian dish benefits from a cucumber salad side dish to counteract the richness of the sauce. If you are serving the satay with rice, try adding fresh, chopped coriander just before serving.

Utensils Coffee grinder or pestle and mortar, mixing bowl, Pyrex or ovenproof bowl, small saucepan, wooden skewers (presoak in water to prevent burning) and a ramekin (small pot)

4 chicken breasts, skinned

Salt and freshly ground black pepper

2 teaspoons cumin seeds (or preground)

4 teaspoons coriander seeds (or preground)

4 tablespoons natural yoghurt

2 teaspoons sweet chilli sauce

1 Slice the chicken into thin strips, about 1cm/½in thick, along the length of the breasts, then season. Grind the cumin and coriander seeds in a coffee grinder or pestle and mortar (if using whole seeds) and mix with the yoghurt and chilli sauce. Stir in the meat and marinade for 2 hours, covered, in the fridge.

Sauce:

250g/9oz smooth peanut butter

6 tablespoons sunflower oil

5 tablespoons sesame oil

5 teaspoons sweet chilli sauce

Salt and freshly ground black pepper

2 To make the sauce, put the peanut butter, oils and chilli sauce in a Pyrex or ovenproof bowl. Melt these ingredients together by placing the bowl over a pan of simmering water. Gently stir with a wooden spoon and season.

Salad:

2 cucumbers

5 spring onions

Salt and freshly ground black pepper

3 limes, juiced

3 For the salad, cut the cucumbers and the spring onions into small, thin strips resembling matchsticks. Season well with salt and pepper and squeeze over the all-important juice from the limes.

4 Preheat the grill to its highest setting. Skewer the meat onto wooden skewers by bending the chicken strips into an 's' shape along each skewer and use a knife to scrape off any excess marinade. Season well and grill each side for 4–5 minutes.

To Serve:

Extra lime quarters

5 To serve, arrange the chicken skewers on warmed plates and place a ramekin (small pot) of peanut sauce by its side. Check the seasoning of the salad and place a small mound on each plate. Garnish with extra lime quarters.

THAI GREEN CURRY

There are many variations of this popular curry. If you are short of time, you can substitute 2 tablespoons of good-quality, ready-made Thai green curry paste instead of making it fresh.

Utensils Large shallow ovenproof casserole or large saucepan and food processor

12 chicken thighs, boned and skinned
1 stick of lemongrass
4 lime leaves (or substitute 4 limes, zested and juiced)

1 Cut each chicken thigh in half and cut the lemongrass stick in half lengthways and finely slice. Remove the vein from the lime leaves (if using) and slice thinly.

2 large green chillies, deseeded and 5 small whole green chillies
1 red onion, chopped
1 tablespoon garlic, chopped
1 large bunch fresh coriander, stem and roots, if available
1 tablespoon ginger or galangal
½ teaspoon tumeric
2 tablespoons each: ground coriander, ground cumin and sunflower oil
2 tablespoons water

2 Finely blend all the paste ingredients together in a food processor.

400ml/16fl oz tin coconut milk
Salt and freshly ground black pepper

3 Pour the coconut milk into the ovenproof casserole. Fill the empty tin with cold water and add it to the pan, stirring. Remove half the liquid and reserve for later. Bring the remaining diluted milk in the pan to the boil and simmer for 5 minutes to reduce. Add the curry paste and simmer for a further 5 minutes. Then add the chicken, remaining coconut milk, lemongrass, lime leaves (or lime zest and juice) and seasoning. Simmer for 30 minutes, uncovered. If you're serving rice, prepare it now (page 120).

30g/1¼oz fresh coriander, chopped
2 tablespoons fish sauce

4 When the chicken is cooked, you can add a little water to the sauce if you prefer a slightly thinner curry. Add the coriander, fish sauce and seasoning as required and remember that fish sauce is very salty.

To Serve:
Rice (page 120) and Braised Mushrooms (page 112)

5 Serve with plenty of rice and Braised Mushrooms.

SMOKED FISH PIE

The hint of smoked fish that we use in this fish pie combines perfectly with the crisp rösti potatoes which have the added flavour of spring onion to make a delicious change. This pie can be made in advance and cooked just before you're ready to eat – the perfect dinner party main course.

Utensils Large and small saucepans, whisk, shallow pan, 24cm/9½in round ovenproof dish and grater

900g/2lb Red Desiree potatoes or any other 'floury' potato such as Maris Piper or White

1 Peel the potatoes and leave them whole. Cook for 12 minutes in boiling, salted water. Strain and leave to cool.

150ml/¼ pint white wine
275ml/10 fl oz fish stock (one small tub)
I bay leaf
675g/1½lb fresh cod
225g/8oz smoked haddock

2 Mix the wine and stock together in a large shallow pan. Add the bay leaf and bring to simmering point. Add the cod and haddock, skin side upwards, and cook for 4 minutes. Take out the fish and leave to cool, saving the cooking liquid. Preheat the oven to 200°C/400°F/Gas 6.

110g/4oz butter
50g/2oz plain flour
175g/6oz Tiger prawns, raw, skinned
3 tablespoons chopped parsley
Salt and freshly ground black pepper

3 Melt half the butter gently in a small saucepan, add the flour and stir well. Gradually whisk in the strained cooking liquid. When all the liquid has been added, turn the heat up slightly and stir until smooth. Remove the skin and bones and flake the fish into the ovenproof serving dish (the pieces can be large because when you add the sauce the fish will break up). Cool slightly, then add the prawns and parsley; season well.

1 bunch spring onions, thinly sliced

4 To make the rösti, thickly grate the potatoes and melt the remaining butter over a low heat in the potato saucepan. Take off the heat and add the potatoes and spring onions. Season well and stir gently to blend, then place evenly on top of the fish. Bake in the oven for 35 minutes.

To Serve:
Cumin Beans (page 116) or a fresh green salad

5 Serve with Cumin Beans or a fresh green salad.

HERB BLINIS

A much-quicker twist on a classic blini, and the addition of fresh herbs makes a far tastier version. This recipe was given to us by an excellent chef, Cherie Marshall, who cooked all the great food for the guests to eat in the green room for *Late Lunch*. Blinis are very versatile: smaller ones can be made into canapés and larger ones may be served as a starter or light lunch. Try topping them with chopped smoked salmon mixed with crème fraîche and chopped dill.

Utensils Food processor (or mixing bowl), large mixing bowl, whisk, large, non-stick frying pan and a metal spatula

1 large bunch dill
1 large bunch tarragon
½ teacup milk
1 egg, plus 1 egg separated

1 In a food processor or by hand, finely chop the herbs, stalks and all. Add the milk, whole egg and egg yolk (save the white to add to three more whites later in the recipe) to the processor or mix in a bowl.

1 teacup plain flour
½ teaspoon baking powder
½ teaspoon bicarbonate of soda
Salt and freshly ground black pepper

2 Add the flour, baking powder and bicarbonate of soda to the mixture and blend again. Then season and pour the mixture into a large bowl.

4 egg whites

3 Whisk the egg whites until firm. Stir a quarter of them into the herb mixture, then fold in the rest of the whites to make a thickish batter.

A little sunflower oil for frying

4 Heat a little sunflower oil in a non-stick frying pan and quickly spoon 2 tablespoons of the herb mixture into the pan. Leave for a few minutes or until the top looks semi-firm and the underside brown. Use a large spatula to flip the pancake over and fry for a few seconds on the other side. Once the technique has been mastered, a few blinis can be cooked at the same time. The mixture should make 6 starter-size blinis.

To Serve:
500g/1lb 2oz smoked salmon or trout
1 lemon or 2 limes
Freshly ground black pepper
1 small pot sour cream
1 small pot fresh salmon eggs (optional)
1 small bunch chives, chopped

5 To serve, the blinis can be made in advance and wrapped together in foil to be reheated gently in the oven (170–180°C/325–350°F/Gas 3–4). Top each one with smoked salmon or trout twisted and piled high, with a squeeze of lemon or lime juice and black pepper, a spoonful of sour cream and – if obtainable – fresh salmon eggs followed by a sprinkling of chives.

Top Man Tip If sour cream is not available, add a good squeeze of lemon juice to double cream and stir well. It hasn't got quite the same acidic flavour but it is an adequate substitute.

CHICKEN WITH A TARRAGON SAUCE

Try this recipe and you'll never buy a precooked version again. Always remember that chicken breasts do not need much cooking. If they're overcooked, they'll become stringy and tough.

Utensils Shallow medium saucepan with lid or sauté pan

570ml/1 pint ready-made chicken stock, available in supermarkets
1 teacup white wine
Salt and freshly ground black pepper
4 medium sized corn-fed chicken breasts, skinned

1 Pour the stock and wine into a shallow medium saucepan or sauté pan and start to simmer over a low heat. Season and add the chicken. Put the lid on and poach (simmer gently) for 10 minutes. If serving with rice, start to cook this now.

30g/1¼oz fresh tarragon

2 While the chicken is cooking, remove all the tarragon leaves from the main stalks and chop them to make about 6 tablespoons. When the chicken is cooked (it should be firm), keep warm by covering with foil or clingfilm.

275ml/½ pint crème fraîche

3 Put the stock on a high heat until it boils. Add half the tarragon and cook for 5 minutes until the stock is reduced by half. Turn down to a simmer, add the crème fraîche and the rest of the tarragon and the poached chicken. Season and simmer for 4–5 minutes to reheat. The sauce should be thick enough to coat the chicken.

To Serve:
Basmati Rice (page 120) and a green vegetable

4 Place each chicken breast on a warmed plate and cover with sauce. Serve with rice and a green vegetable.

CHICKEN WITH A LEMONGRASS AND COCONUT SAUCE

Serves 4

Preparation and Cooking Time:
1 hour

Although quite a bit of chopping is needed at the beginning of this recipe, once it's in the pan it is very straightforward. The spices combine well together to give an amazingly rich pungent sauce. If lime leaves are difficult to obtain, they could be replaced with lime zest. The tamarind gives a unique citrus flavouring and it is worth looking around for. Barts Spices are available in most supermarkets and they produce an excellent tamarind paste.

Utensils Coffee grinder or pestle and mortar, grater and large ovenproof casserole

2 red chillies
2 lemongrass stalks
5 lime leaves
1 tablespoon brown sugar
3 teaspoons cumin seeds (or preground)
2cm/¾in piece fresh ginger

1 First prepare the spices: cut the chillies in half, remove the seeds and chop finely. Slice the lemongrass in half lengthwise; chop finely. Remove the vein from the lime leaves and finely slice. Measure out the sugar, grind the cumin seeds in a coffee grinder or pestle and mortar, and grate the ginger without removing the skin.

12 chicken thighs, boned and skinned
A little sunflower oil
Salt and freshly ground black pepper

2 Cut each chicken thigh into three pieces. Heat the oil in a large ovenproof casserole and brown the chicken pieces a few at a time; season. Remove the chicken and set to one side.

1 teacup fresh chicken stock
250ml/8 fl oz tinned coconut milk

3 Put all the spices in the casserole and heat through for 1 minute over a medium heat. Add the chicken stock and coconut milk, scraping all the bits from the bottom of the casserole. Return the chicken to the pan.

2 limes
2 teaspoons tamarind paste

4 Add the lime zest to the pan, along with the juice of 1 lime. Stir in the tamarind paste. Simmer, uncovered, for 30 minutes. (If serving with rice (page 120), start cooking it 20 minutes before the chicken is ready). Check the seasoning and squeeze the juice from the remaining lime over the chicken just before serving.

Salsa:
1 mango and 1 red onion, chopped
Lots of fresh mint
2 dessertspoons natural yoghurt
Salt and black pepper

5 Serve with plenty of rice and the salsa.

ROASTED VEGETABLE LASAGNE

Serves 4

Preparation and Cooking Time:
1 hour

Utensils 2–3 large baking trays, 1 small baking tray, grater, hand blender or food processor, large saucepan (optional) and a large ovenproof dish (approximately 24cm/9½in)

700g/1½lb vine or plum tomatoes
A little olive oil
Salt and freshly ground black pepper
2 red and 2 yellow peppers

1 Preheat the oven to 220°C/425°F/Gas 7. Halve the tomatoes. Place on a large baking tray, drizzle with olive oil and season. Cut the peppers in half lengthwise and remove the seeds and stalks with a sharp knife. Cut each half again lengthwise into 4, then into 2cm/¾in squares. Place on another baking tray. Drizzle with olive oil and season.

3 medium courgettes

2 Cut the courgettes into thin slices lengthwise and then again into 2–3cm/¾–1½in squares.

3 medium red onions
A little balsamic vinegar

3 Cut the onions in half, cutting through the roots and then into eighths. Drizzle with olive oil and season. If you have another baking tray, use it to roast the courgettes; if not, they can be roasted after the peppers. Roast the tomatoes for 20 minutes, the peppers for 15 minutes and the onions with the courgettes for 8 minutes or until slightly browned. Drizzle the roasted vegetables with balsamic vinegar and leave to cool.

60g/2½oz pine nuts

4 While the oven is still hot, brown the pine nuts on a small baking tray for 3–4 minutes (keep an eye on them, as they blacken easily). Turn the oven down to 190°C/375°F/Gas 5.

60g/2½oz Parmigiano Reggiano cheese
150g/5oz Cheddar cheese
6–8 sheets fresh lasagne pasta

5 Grate the cheeses. Blend the cooked, whole tomatoes, seeds and all, to a smooth purée with a hand blender or food processor; season well.

6 If you have time, cover the pasta with boiling water to blanch. Leave for 5 minutes and drain on a clean tea towel. Otherwise the pasta can be used straight from the packet, but blanching gives a better result.

250g/9oz ricotta or cream cheese

7 Carefully mix all the roasted vegetables together and season. Spoon half the vegetables into the base of an ovenproof dish, sprinkle with pine nuts, cover with half the tomato sauce and season. Next, layer with a third of the cheeses, dot with ricotta or cream cheese, season and cover evenly with pasta. Repeat the layering process.

To Serve:
A green salad or rocket and Parmesan shavings

8 Sprinkle evenly with the remaining cheeses and bake for 30 minutes until golden brown and bubbling. Serve with a green salad or rocket and shaved Parmesan.

GRILLED HALIBUT WITH MONTPELLIER BUTTER

Montpellier butter will go equally well with any other grilled or fried fish. It can be made in advance and frozen. Here we use halibut, which is a firm, white fleshy fish at its best all year around except May, June and July.

Utensils Mixing bowl, small saucepan, pastry brush and medium baking tray

3 fillets tinned anchovies
2 tablespoons chopped flat leaf parsley
½ clove garlic
1 medium lemon, juiced
110g/4oz unsalted butter at room temperature, plus a little extra for grilling
Salt and freshly ground black pepper

1 Finely chop the anchovies, parsley and garlic. Mix together the lemon juice and butter in a bowl then add the chopped ingredients. Season, bearing in mind that the anchovies are already salty.

2 Lay a large piece of clingfilm flat on a surface and fold it over to make a double thickness. Scrape the butter onto the clingfilm and roll it up into a long sausage shape (approximately 10cm/4in long) and twist it at each end to tighten. Put it in the fridge to harden for approximately 30 minutes. If you're serving vegetables, cook them now as the fish will only take a few minutes to finish.

4 x 175g/6oz halibut slices

3 Turn the grill up to its highest setting. Place the halibut on a baking tray, melt a little butter in a saucepan and brush it over the surface. Season and grill for 4 minutes.

4 When the fish is cooked, place a thick slice of butter (about ½cm/¼in) on top of each piece of fish and put back under the grill for a few seconds until the butter has melted.

To Serve:
Lemon Baked Fennel (page 117) or Puréed Fennel (page 122)

5 Serve on hot plates with Lemon Baked or Puréed Fennel.

JOHNNY HERBERT'S TEMPURA COD WITH OVEN ROASTED CHIPS

Serves 4
Preparation and Cooking Time:
25 minutes

Johnny Herbert's favourite recipe for Tempura Cod combines perfectly with our easy Oven Roasted Chips.

Utensils Two large baking trays, large, deep saucepan suitable for deep frying, mixing bowl, whisk, small bowl and serving dish

A little olive oil
900g/2lb floury potatoes, such as Red Desiree or Maris Piper
Salt and freshly ground black pepper

1 Preheat the oven to 200°C/400°F/Gas 6. Pour a little olive oil onto a large baking tray and warm the tray in the oven. Wash the potatoes, cut into quarters, then cut each quarter into chunky segments to make the chips. Season and put on the hot baking tray. Bake in the oven for 20 minutes.

2 litres/3¾ pints vegetable oil
110g/4oz plain flour
110g/4oz cornflour
350ml/12 fl oz iced soda water

2 Pour all the vegetable oil into the deep pan, making sure it is only half full and heat. In a bowl, mix together the flour and cornflour. Whisk in the iced soda water. Don't worry about any lumps: these actually improve the texture of the batter, which should be made and used straight away.

700g/1½lb fresh cod, skinned and cut into 4cm/1½in cubes
A little extra seasoned plain flour (to coat the fish)

3 To fry the fish, the oil temperature must reach 190°C/375°F. If you don't have a thermometer, test the temperature by throwing a piece of bread into the oil. The oil is ready if the bread takes only 1 minute to brown. Roll each piece of fish in seasoned flour, then dip into the batter and carefully drop it straight into the pan. Do a batch of fish pieces at a time – they will only take a few minutes to cook – and when they're golden brown, transfer to a baking tray and place in the oven.

4 tablespoons good-quality mayonnaise
1 medium lemon, juiced

4 While the fish is cooking, mix the mayonnaise with the lemon juice and season well.

5 When the chips are ready they will be crispy. To keep them warm, tip them onto a serving dish lined with kitchen paper and keep warm in a low oven (150°C/300°F/Gas 2).

To Serve:
Parsley sprigs, lemon wedges and extra sea salt

6 Roll the fish on kitchen paper, then serve a mound of crisp cod on each plate and garnish with a sprig of parsley and a wedge of lemon. Serve the mayonnaise and chips separately with extra sea salt.

ROCKET SALAD WITH PARMA HAM AND TRUFFLE OIL

Serves 4
Preparation Time: 5–10 minutes

Rocket, a peppery green herb (often mistaken for a salad leaf), is now readily available everywhere but at its best from May to September. This salad has the unique flavouring of truffle oil. Good truffle oil, which has a powerful and strong flavour, can be obtained from Italian delis but it is very expensive. The type found at supermarkets is much lighter and completely different, and it's what we recommend for this salad. Another bonus: it's also slightly cheaper! If all the ingredients are prepared in advance for this recipe, it's just a question of putting them together and serving at the last minute. This dish makes a great starter or light lunch with crusty bread or herby foccacia.

Utensils Small baking tray and potato peeler

1 Preheat the oven to 200°C/400°F/Gas 6.

75g/3oz pine nuts **2** Arrange the pine nuts evenly on a small baking tray. When the oven is hot, put the pine nuts in to brown for about 3 minutes. Keep a close eye on them as they will turn from a pale brown to black very quickly.

250g/9oz rocket **3** Wash and dry the rocket, picking off any long stems.

75g/3oz Parmigiano Reggiano cheese **4** Use a potato peeler to create long shavings of Parmesan.

110g/4oz Parma ham **5** Cut the Parma ham into small strips of about 2 x 5cm/¾ x 2in and reserve in layers of clingfilm.

A drizzle of truffle oil
Salt and freshly ground black pepper **6** To serve, arrange the rocket on large individual plates. Drizzle with truffle oil, season well and, using a spoon and fork, toss the leaves to coat them with oil. Arrange the ham on top, then sprinkle with pine nuts and pile cheese on top.

Top Man Tip As an alternative to truffle oil, try a good extra virgin olive or basil oil.

SEA BASS WITH ASIAN GREENS

Serves 4
Preparation and Cooking Time:
35 minutes

This is an adaptation of an Alastair Little recipe. Bass is particularly good to use in this recipe as once cooked, its skin will be crispy and the white flesh succulent. If you want to substitute another fish use sole, turbot, halibut or brill (their flesh does not break up during cooking either). Bass is not in season from January through to June.

Utensils Grater, mixing bowl, tweezers, large ovenproof frying pan, wok and palette knife

2 tablespoons soy sauce
1 lemon, juiced
1 teaspoon grated fresh ginger
1 clove garlic, chopped
2 red chillies, deseeded and thinly sliced

1 In a bowl, mix together the soy sauce, lemon juice, ginger, garlic and chillies.

150g/5oz pak choi leaves
200g/7oz baby spinach leaves
1 bunch spring onions
125g/4½oz shiitake mushrooms

2 Slice the pak choi into thick 2cm/¾in pieces. Wash the spinach. Cut the spring onions diagonally into 1cm/½in slices and thinly slice the mushrooms. Preheat the oven to 200°C/400°F/Gas 6.

4 x 225g/8oz sea bass fillets
A little seasoned flour

3 Trim the sea bass fillets and check that all the bones have been removed. Tweezers can be used to remove any rogue bones. Sprinkle a little seasoned flour onto each fillet. If serving rice, cook it now.

75g/3oz butter

4 Melt 50g/2oz butter in a large frying pan. When hot, add the fish, skin side down, and leave for 3 minutes. Then place the whole pan in the oven for 5 minutes. If you don't have a pan that can go directly into the oven, use a heated baking tray.

Salt and freshly ground black pepper

5 While the fish is cooking, heat a wok. Add the pak choi, spring onions, spinach and mushrooms, and simply pour over the soy mix. Season and stir fry until the spinach has wilted and the mushrooms are cooked, then add the remaining butter.

To Serve:
A little chilli oil and rice

6 When the vegetables have wilted and the sauce has reduced a little, season and spoon onto warm plates. Using a palette knife, place the fish on top of the vegetables. If wished, a little chilli oil can be drizzled over. This can be served with rice.

PETE TONG'S SPAGHETTI VONGOLE

DJ Pete Tong gave us this recipe for Spaghetti alle Vongole. If you can get them, Pete suggests you use Sicilian Pachino cherry tomatoes and Veraci clams.

Utensils Large saucepan and large frying pan

900g/2lb Veraci clams
Salt and freshly ground black pepper

1 Wash the clams thoroughly and place them in a saucepan. Cover with a few inches of water and add some salt. Put the lid on and steam over a medium heat for 5–10 minutes until the clams open up. Remove about three quarters of the clams from their shells, leaving the 'best looking' ones to one side. Keep the water you've used for steaming the clams to one side as you'll be using it again later.

Extra virgin olive oil
3 medium garlic cloves, chopped
½ dry red chilli, chopped
15g/¾oz fresh parsley, chopped

2 Pour the olive oil into a frying pan over a medium heat and add the garlic, chopped chilli and some of the parsley. Cook until the garlic lightly browns.

6 cherry tomatoes, halved
¼ glass of white wine

3 Add the tomatoes and the clams to the pan. Cook over a medium heat for about 10 minutes, then add half a glass of the strained water from the clams and the wine.

225g/8oz spaghetti

4 Place the pasta in a saucepan of boiling salted water (use some of the water from the steamed clams) for 10–12 minutes or until 'al dente' (firm to the bite). Let the sauce reduce for 5 minutes.

5 To serve, drain and pour the pasta into the frying pan with the sauce. Add the remaining chopped parsley and serve hot.

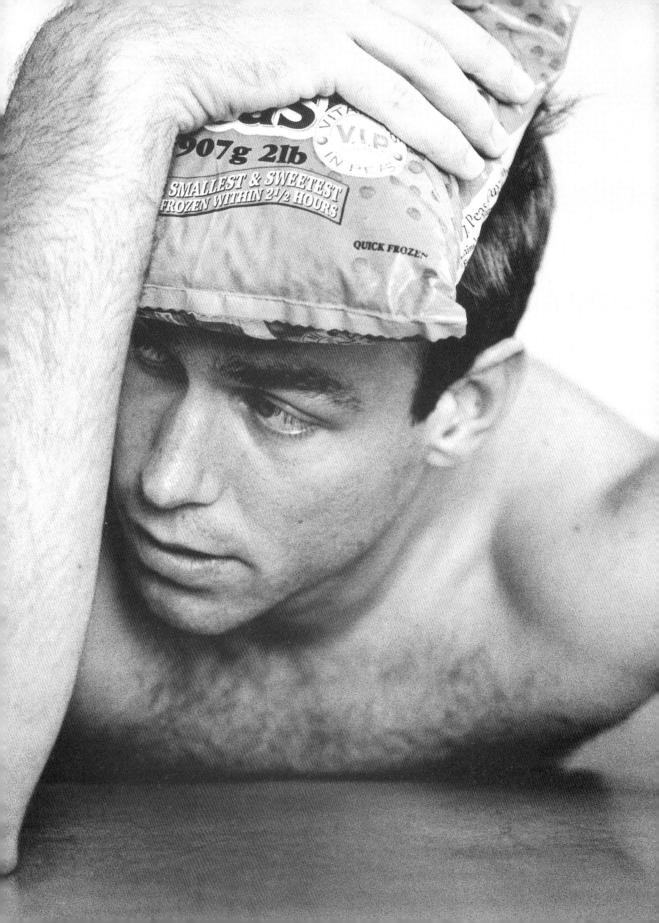

the recovery

One way of curing a hangover

is to eat the right foods and to re-hydrate your body with the right liquids. Drink plenty of mineral water and you'll need vitamins, particularly Vitamin B, so replenish your battered system with a Vitamin-packed Smoothie. Familiar, straightforward food prepared with a little oil can also provide some relief and make you feel more like your normal self. If all else fails, try our quick spicy Bloody Mary – it will soon put the spring back in your step!

Serves 2
Preparation and Cooking Time:
5 minutes

THE CLASSIC BLT

A classic hangover cure.

Utensils Frying pan

8 slices smoked streaky bacon
4 slices granary or brown bread
Good-quality mayonnaise

1 Fry the bacon in its own fat in a frying pan over a medium heat or grill for 3–4 minutes, turning once. Toast the bread and spread thickly with mayonnaise.

2 medium size tomatoes
4 Little Gem lettuce leaves
Salt and freshly ground black pepper

2 Slice the tomatoes and layer with the lettuce onto the bread. Season well.

3 When the bacon is crisp, add it to the sandwich.

FRIED EGGS WITH HAM AND CRUSHED POTATOES

Serves 2
Preparation and Cooking Time:
25 minutes

Utensils Small saucepan, frying pan and spatula

450g/1lb (about 3) Red Desiree or new potatoes, peeled and cut into 2cm/¾in cubes

1 Put the potatoes into the saucepan and cover with slightly salted water. Bring to the boil and simmer for 5 minutes, uncovered. When the potatoes are just soft, drain them. Preheat the oven to 150°C/300°F/Gas 20

2 tablespoons olive oil
½ medium size onion, finely chopped
2 tablespoons red wine vinegar
Salt and freshly ground black pepper

2 Heat the oil in the frying pan, add the potatoes and fry until golden brown. Add the onion and red wine vinegar (which will soon reduce); season. Turn out onto a plate. Using a fork, roughly crush the potato and onion mix; season as necessary.

Butter for frying
4–5 thickly-cut slices smoked ham

3 Melt the butter in the frying pan, add the potatoes and push them into the shape of a 'cake'. Fry for a few minutes until brown, then turn over using a spatula. Continue doing this until your potato cake has a golden crust. Remove and keep warm in a the oven. Arrange the ham on plates.

2 free range eggs

4 Melt some more butter in the frying pan and gently fry the lightly seasoned eggs. Baste the eggs with the butter until the yolks are opaque.

Chopped fresh parsley, to garnish

5 To serve, spoon the potatoes onto the ham, top each serving with an egg and sprinkle with chopped parsley.

BLOODY MARY

⅕ vodka to ⅘ fresh tomato
juice
Fresh horseradish
Good squeeze lemon juice
Worcester sauce
Sprinkling of celery salt
Dash of Tabasco

1   In a tall glass, mix together the vodka and fresh tomato juice. The rest of the ingredients should be stirred in according to taste. Bear in mind that the celery salt is a very important ingredient. Serve chilled.

Serves 2
Preparation and Cooking Time:
10–15 minutes, chilled for
as long as possible

BUBBLE AND SQUEAK

This is really a recipe for leftovers as cooking it from scratch would mean many pots and pans! Try a big plateful for some comfort; it really works! The parsnips go deliciously well with the cabbage and potatoes. Add whatever leftover vegetables you have to this dish – peas, swede, whatever you fancy.

Utensils Large non-stick frying pan and mixing bowl

175g/6oz parsnips, cooked
150g/5oz potatoes, cooked
1 onion
A little vegetable oil
Salt and freshly ground black
pepper
175g/6oz green cabbage,
cooked

1   Mash the parsnips and potatoes together in a bowl and season. Slice the onion. Heat the oil in a large frying pan and fry the onion until soft. Season and add, with the cabbage, to the parsnips and potatoes.

A little flour

2   Season again and mould the mixture into 4 rounds of about 7.5 x 2cm/3 x ¾in. Cover and chill for as long as you can. Lightly flour the individual cakes.

A little butter

3   Heat the butter in a large non-stick frying pan and fry the cakes on both sides for a few minutes until golden brown.

To Serve:
Ham and fried eggs

4   Serve with ham and fried eggs.

THE FRY-UP

Utensils Large frying pan and a small baking tray

A little butter
225g/8oz pork and herb
sausages

1 Preheat the oven to 190°C/375°F/Gas 5. Over a medium heat and in a large frying pan, brown the sausages in a little butter. Place on a baking tray, cover with foil and cook in the oven for about 20 minutes.

4 plum tomatoes
Salt and freshly ground black
pepper
Dried oregano

2 Halve the tomatoes and dot a little butter on each half. Season well and sprinkle with a little oregano. Place in the oven with the sausages.

225g/8oz smoked back bacon,
organic or streaky (choose
the best quality, page 159)

3 After 20 minutes, heat a large frying pan over a medium heat. Fry the bacon for 4–5 minutes and then keep it warm in the oven.

8 free range medium size eggs

4 Turn the heat down to low and, if needed, add more butter to the pan. Crack in the eggs and baste by tilting and spooning the fat over the egg yolks. (Remember that all eggs should be cooked gently over a low heat.) After about 3 minutes they should be ready – very lightly crisp around the edges and soft in the middle.

To Serve:
Mustard and tomato ketchup

5 To serve, if necessary drain on kitchen paper and serve on hot plates with mustard and tomato ketchup.

VITAMIN-PACKED SMOOTHIE

Utensils Hand blender or food processor

Raspberries
Strawberries
Orange juice
Bananas
Vanilla yoghurt
Wheatgerm, for sprinkling

1 Blend together all the ingredients apart from the wheatgerm using a hand blender or food processor. Pour into a tall glass and sprinkle with wheatgerm. Serve chilled.

Top Man Tip When nursing a hangover, you need to replenish your system with vitamin B and C. All these fruits are bursting with the right vitamins – the wheatgerm is great for Vitamin B.

chapter ten

mange tout

Many vegetable recipes

not only stand up well on their own but can transform a simple piece of grilled fish or meat into a delicious and interesting meal when you're strapped for time. Try to use seasonal vegetables and find the freshest available to ensure the best flavour. Don't worry about getting the exact ingredients if they aren't easy to come by – experiment with all types as vegetables are very versatile.

Serves 4
Preparation and Cooking Time:
30 minutes

SAFFRON MASH

This mash is delicious just the way it is, but if you want to make a wickedly decadent version, replace the milk with double cream!

Utensils 1 small and 1 medium saucepan, and a masher or ricer

900g/2lb Maris Piper or White potatoes

1 very large pinch of saffron
1 teacup full fat milk
25g/1oz butter

Salt and freshly ground black pepper

1   Peel and halve the potatoes and place them in the medium saucepan. Cover with cold, salted water and boil, uncovered, for 20–25 minutes.

2   Put the saffron, milk and butter into the small saucepan and heat gently to infuse. Take off the heat when the butter has melted and leave to one side.

3   When the potatoes are cooked (they should be soft – test them with a sharp knife), drain off the water and return them to the saucepan. Mash well then pour in the creamy saffron liquid. Season and continue to mash until there are no lumps.

4   The mash can be served straight away or it can be left to keep warm in its saucepan with a lid on top or covered with clingfilm.

TEDDY SHERINGHAM'S MUSTARD MASH

Mashed potatoes, 'mash', is everywhere now. The best ever mash is passed through a mouli or a sieve. Another handy tool to have in your kitchen, which is great for mashing is a 'ricer', which is like a huge garlic press. But if you use the right potatoes, such as Maris Piper or Whites, a good old masher with plenty of arm power will suffice. Never process potatoes as they'll turn instantly into glue. This mash recipe is Teddy's favourite.

Utensils 1 medium saucepan and a masher or ricer

900g/2lb Maris Piper or White potatoes

1 Peel and halve the potatoes and place them in a medium saucepan. Cover with cold, salted water and boil, uncovered, for 20–25 minutes.

2 When the potatoes are cooked (they should be soft – test them with a sharp knife), drain off the water, return them to the saucepan and mash well.

50g/2oz butter
6 tablespoons double cream
2 heaped tablespoons grainy mustard
2 heaped tablespoons Dijon mustard
Salt and freshly ground black pepper

3 Add the butter, cream, mustards and seasoning. Continue to mash until all the lumps have been removed.

MUSHROOMS EN PAPILLOTE

Any variety of mushroom can be used in this recipe. Although we've specified using portabello and chestnut here, try substituting the portabello with wild mushrooms for an interesting earthy flavour. Prepackaged mixed wild mushrooms are readily available in most supermarkets but make sure you clean them well as they can be gritty. Brush off any dirt rather than rinsing them with water which tends to make them soggy. Do try portabello though as they have a fantastic flavour which is not to be missed.

Utensils Tin foil, baking tray and spatula

1   Preheat oven to 190°C/375°F/Gas 5.

250g/9oz portabello mushrooms
250g/9oz chestnut mushrooms

2   Slice the mushrooms into ½cm/¼in slices.

3   Tear 4 pieces of tin foil into large (about 25cm/10in) squares and pile equal quantities of mushrooms onto each piece.

Salt and freshly ground black pepper
4 sprigs tarragon
A little olive oil

4   Season each mushroom pile, top with a sprig of tarragon and drizzle with olive oil. Wrap the foil tightly around the mushrooms to form 4 'parcels'.

5   Place on a baking tray and bake in the oven for 30 minutes.

6   To serve, unwrap each parcel and, using a spatula, slide the mushrooms carefully onto hot plates and pour the cooking juices over each pile.

Top Man Tip To make serving easier, place the parcels directly on serving plates and let each guest open up their own.

BRAISED RED CABBAGE WITH APPLE

This simple dish is delicious eaten with pretty much anything and its deep purple tone looks great on the plate. The sharpness complements rich, luxurious flavours of dishes such as roasted pork and duck. You can prepare it and leave it cooking slowly in the oven, and forget about it for an hour.

Utensils Medium (20cm/8in) ovenproof dish with lid

1   Preheat the oven to 150°C/325°F/Gas Mark 3.

1 small red cabbage 2   Cut the cabbage into quarters, cut away the core and shred the rest into thin ½cm/¼in slices.

2 Granny Smith apples 3   Peel the apples, cut into quarters and remove the cores. Slice thinly.
1 medium onion   Peel and thinly slice the onion.

Salt and freshly ground black 4   Layer the cabbage, apples and onion into an ovenproof dish, adding
pepper   plenty of seasoning as you go.

4 tablespoons water 5   Mix together the water, red wine vinegar and sugar. Pour over the
4 tablespoons red wine vinegar   vegetable and fruit layers.
2 tablespoons sugar

6   Cover with a lid and cook in the oven for 1–1½ hours or until the whole mass is soft and reduced in bulk.

7   You can serve the cabbage immediately or reheat it in a medium oven (170°C/325°F/Gas 3) for 20 minutes provided it is covered with a lid. Check for seasoning and add a little more water if necessary as it shouldn't be dry.

Top Man Tip If your oven is already full, you can cook this on the hob. Melt a knob of butter in a frying pan, add the ingredients and gently cook over a low heat without a lid.

Serves 2

Preparation and Cooking time:
40 minutes

ROASTED VEGETABLES WITH COUSCOUS

Seasoned well, roasted vegetables taste outstanding and have the added bonus of being packed with vitamins and minerals. They are extremely versatile and can be served either as an accompaniment or with couscous as a main course. This particular recipe is perfect for summer when the ingredients are in abundance and at their best.

Utensils:
Large baking tray and medium saucepan with lid

1 aubergine

1 Preheat the oven to 200°C/400°F/Gas 6. Cut the aubergine in half lengthways, cut each piece in half again and into 4cm/1½in squares.

1 red and 1 yellow pepper

2 Cut the peppers in half lengthways, remove the seeds and stalks, then cut into 4cm/1½in squares.

2 red onions

3 Cut the onions in half through the core, then peel and slice them lengthways into 2cm/¾in lengths.

Olive oil
2 sprigs of thyme
Salt and freshly ground black pepper

4 Place the prepared vegetables directly onto a baking tray. Drizzle generously with olive oil (make sure all the vegetables are coated) and sprinkle on the thyme sprigs. Season well and place in the oven for 20–25 minutes.

2 medium courgettes
110g/4oz pitted black olives

5 Cut the courgettes into 2cm/¾in slices and season. When the other vegetables have been in the oven for 15 minutes, add the courgettes and olives and roast for 5–10 minutes. They should all be touching the bottom of the baking tray to get the benefit of the heat and to add colour and flavour.

1½ pints vegetable stock
225g/8oz couscous

6 Meanwhile, make the vegetable stock according to the directions on the bouillon powder package in a medium saucepan and bring it to the boil. Add the couscous and cover with a lid. Take off the heat and leave to stand for 5 minutes.

Balsamic vinegar, for drizzling

7 Test the courgettes with a sharp knife after 5 minutes' cooking; they should be just cooked, crunchy but not soggy. When cooked, drizzle with a little balsamic vinegar and season well.

8 To serve, lightly fork through the couscous to break it up, pile it onto a plate and top with a generous mound of vegetables.

Serves 4

Preparation and Cooking Time:

15–20 minutes

SAVOY CABBAGE WITH PANCETTA

Pancetta is the Italian version of our bacon, so you could use regular bacon if it is unavailable. However, there is nothing quite like the combination of the fresh tasty cabbage and the smoky pork flavour of the pancetta. Like all the vegetable recipes in this chapter, this will go well with any grilled meat or fish.

Utensils Large frying pan or wok

I medium size Savoy cabbage
225g/8oz pancetta
or smoked streaky bacon in
one thick piece

1   Cut the cabbage into quarters, remove the core and shred into thin slices. Chop the pancetta or bacon into ½cm/¼in chunks.

Knob of butter
Salt and freshly ground black
pepper

2   Melt the butter in a large frying pan or wok over a low heat. Add the bacon and fry lightly. Then add the cabbage with a little water and season well. Gradually the cabbage will wilt down. If it gets a bit dry, just add a little water and extra butter. Cook until soft (this should take approximately 10–15 minutes).

BRAISED MUSHROOMS

Louise created this dish with one of the celebrity cooks on Channel 4's *Late Lunch* to accompany a Thai Chicken Stir Fry. It goes well with almost any Thai dish as it is very light and fresh. The Chinese rice wine gives it an unusual flavour and it can be found in most major supermarkets in the specialist food section. If you can't get it, substitute a light sherry. Morels are also found in the specialist section at supermarkets or in a good Italian deli. Their flavour is quite unique.

Utensils Small heatproof bowl, large frying pan or wok

50g/2oz dried morels

1 Place the morels in a bowl and cover with boiling water. Leave for 15 minutes. Drain, but keep the soaking liquid.

110g/4oz shiitake mushrooms
110g/4oz chestnut mushrooms
4 spring onions

2 Slice the mushrooms about 1cm/½in thick and slice the spring onions diagonally, keeping the white and green colours separately.

3 tablespoons extra virgin olive oil
2 tablespoons Chinese rice wine
4 teaspoons soy sauce
Salt and freshly ground black pepper

3 Heat the oil gently in a large frying pan or wok, add all the mushrooms and the white of the spring onions. Stir for a few seconds and then add the rice wine, soy sauce and a little of the mushroom soaking liquid. Season and leave to cook for approximately 10 minutes.

4 To serve, season and sprinkle with the green part of the spring onions. This dish will keep warm for a while, covered, in a low oven.

POTATO GRATIN

The remarkable gratin is a French classic dish normally cooked plain or 'Savoyarde' with cheese on top. This one has some interesting additions. It goes well with pretty much everything, particularly as an alternative to roast potatoes with a roast cut of meat.

Utensils Small heatproof bowl, large saucepan, and a large gratin dish or medium ovenproof dish

15g/¾oz dried porcini mushrooms
700g/1½lb Red Desiree or other potatoes
1 medium onion
1 clove garlic
3 sprigs thyme or sage

1 Preheat the oven to 180°C/350°F/Gas 4. In a bowl cover the mushrooms with boiling water. Peel and slice the potatoes and onion as thinly as you can. Peel and chop the garlic and pick the herbs from the main stalks.

275ml/½ pint full fat milk
275ml/½ pint whipping cream
Salt and freshly ground black pepper

2 Gently heat the milk and cream in a large saucepan and season well. When it starts to simmer, add the other ingredients and cook over a low heat for 4 minutes, stirring occasionally. This begins the cooking process and therefore the potatoes won't take so long in the oven.

3 Pour the mixture into a large gratin or medium ovenproof dish. Cover with foil and bake in the oven for 30 minutes.

4 Serve when very hot. (The gratin can be made in advance and reheated in the oven when needed.)

Top Man Tip Try alternative ingredients such as Jerusalem artichokes, parsnips, sweet potatoes, celeriac or fresh wild mushrooms and, for a decadent alternative, dried morels. You can also use any type of fresh herbs. Try tarragon or rosemary.

VEGETABLE PUREE

A purée is a great alternative to plain boiled vegetables and is extremely versatile. Any vegetables can be used but remember that seasoning is very important. Purées can be easily and successfully reheated. In this version, the roasted garlic gives a different dimension to the flavours.

Utensils Small baking tray, large saucepan, and a food processor or hand blender

4 cloves garlic

1 Preheat the oven to 150°C/300°F/Gas 2. Place the unpeeled cloves of garlic on a small baking tray and bake for 30 minutes.

1 swede, about 900g/2lb
1 celeriac, about 900g/2lb

2 Meanwhile, peel the swede and celeriac using a small, very sharp knife or peeler to take away the thin outer layer. Cut into small 4cm/1½in chunks and place in a large saucepan of cold, salted water. Bring to the boil and simmer for approximately 20 minutes.

3 Check the vegetables with the tip of a knife. When they're very soft, drain and put them back in the saucepan to steam for a few seconds. Then use a food processor or hand blender to purée them until smooth.

2 tablespoons crème fraîche
A good squeeze of lemon
Salt and freshly ground black pepper

4 Cut the ends away from the garlic and squeeze the puréed soft pulp into the vegetables. Add the crème fraîche and lemon juice, season well and blend again.

5 The purée can either be eaten immediately or kept hot for a while covered in clingfilm. To reheat, place the baking tray, covered in foil, in a medium oven (180°C/350°F/Gas 4) for 20 minutes.

Top Man Tip Any root vegetables can be used, but remember not to use a blender for potatoes: only use a masher. If potatoes are blended, the starch that comes out of them will cause the purée to resemble glue.

PEAS WITH ROCKET AND SPRING ONIONS

When you are looking for an accompanying vegetable that is speedy but slightly different, this recipe is for you. It's great with a simply cooked piece of meat or fish. Try it with fresh peas (available June–July).

Utensils Large saucepan and small bowl

450g/1lb bag frozen petits pois
1 bunch spring onions, cut to approximately 6cm/2½in in length, trimmed and peeled as necessary
30g/1¼oz rocket
4 or 5 sprigs of mint
1 teaspoon Marigold vegetable stock granules
Salt and freshly ground black pepper

1 Place the peas, spring onions, rocket and mint in a saucepan and pour over enough boiling water to just cover them. Add the stock granules and season. Stir and simmer, uncovered, over a medium heat for 3–4 minutes.

1 tablespoon flour
25g/1oz butter at room temperature

2 Meanwhile, mix the flour and butter together thoroughly in a bowl and add to the peas. Stir well. After 2–3 minutes, the liquid will thicken. Place over a low heat, stirring gently, for a couple of minutes to cook out the flour. Check the seasoning again as a little more salt may be needed. This dish can be held for a while and reheated as necessary in the same saucepan.

Top Man Tip Flour and butter (beurre manié) can be used to thicken any sauce when a rich taste is needed.

CUMIN BEANS

This remarkably simple recipe goes with absolutely anything. It is important to keep the beans slightly crunchy and not overcooked.

Utensils Heat proof bowl, coffee grinder or pestle and mortar (optional) and large saucepan

2 medium vine or plum tomatoes
½ medium red onion

1 Skin the tomatoes by placing them in a bowl of boiling water for 1 minute. Check the skins for peeling then plunge into very cold water. Halve and remove the seeds with a teaspoon; roughly dice. Halve the onion, remove the root and slice thinly.

250g/9oz fine French beans
2 teaspoons cumin seeds (or preground)
Salt and freshly ground black pepper

2 Remove the stalks from the end of the beans. If not using preground, grind the cumin in the coffee grinder or pestle and mortar. Boil a large saucepan of salted water and throw in the beans. Leave to simmer over a low heat for 3–4 minutes, then drain.

Extra virgin olive oil (or olive oil)

3 Put the beans back into the same pan, mix in the other prepared ingredients and add a generous drizzle of extra virgin or ordinary olive oil and seasoning.

4 To serve, pile onto a warmed serving plate or into a bowl.

Top Man Tip Pick the beans by hand because when the top is peeled off, the stringy part will automatically come away from the side.

LEMON BAKED FENNEL

Utensils Medium saucepan with lid and metal handle

2 medium fennel bulbs

1 Preheat the oven to 190°C/375°F/Gas 5. Cut the fennel lengthways and slice thinly (you can trim off a thin slice from the root end, if needed).

Large knob of butter
1 medium lemon, juiced
3 tablespoons cold water
Salt and freshly ground black pepper

2 Melt the butter in a medium saucepan. When foaming, add the fennel, lemon juice, water and seasoning. Leave for 1 minute to regain the heat, put the lid on and place the whole pan in the oven for 25 minutes.

3 The fennel should be served just cooked with a slight bite. Serve in a warmed serving dish or as a bed for an oven baked piece of fish.

Top Man Tip Be careful of the hot saucepan handle when removing the baked fennel from the oven. As one of our witty testers suggested, put a pizza in the top part of the oven to have on standby if you don't like it! Needless to say, he did.

SPINACH WITH CREAM CHEESE

Utensils Large frying pan and kitchen tongs

1 large knob of butter
225g/8oz baby spinach leaves

1 Melt the butter in the frying pan over a medium heat. When foaming, add the spinach, stalks and all. Using tongs, stir and turn over the leaves so that they cook evenly.

75g/3oz cream cheese
Salt and freshly ground black pepper
Freshly grated nutmeg

2 After a few minutes, when wilted, add the cream cheese, plenty of seasoning and a few scrapings of nutmeg. Using tongs, mix well and serve immediately.

Top Man Tip If you're cooking for more than two people, you can cook the spinach as above in batches, keeping it warm in the oven (170°C/325°F/Gas 3).

SPICED PUY LENTILS

Puy lentils are considered the finest of all lentils for flavour and are grown on the organic soil around Le Puy in France. They are quick to cook, unlike ordinary lentils, which seem to take forever. This recipe has the flavourings of South East Asia and makes the perfect accompaniment to roasted fish.

Utensils Pestle and mortar (optional) and medium saucepan

½ medium onion
1 clove garlic
2 red chillies
1 teaspoon cardamom seeds
(taken from about 3 green
pods, see method)
Knob of butter

1 Chop the onion and garlic finely. Halve the chillies, remove the seeds and chop finely. Crush the cardamom pods with the back of a spoon or in a pestle and mortar and gather the little black seeds. Melt the butter in a medium saucepan, add the onion and garlic, along with the chillies and cardamom seeds, and cook over a low heat for 1 minute.

1 x 400g/14oz tin chopped
tomatoes
350g/12oz puy lentils
Salt and freshly ground black
pepper
4 teacups fish stock or water

2 Add the tomatoes, lentils and seasoning and turn the heat up to simmering point. Add the fish stock or water and continue to simmer steadily for 20–25 minutes, uncovered, or until the lentils are tender. (Puy lentils, unlike other varieties, will hold their shape.)

3 tablespoons fish sauce
1 medium lemon, juiced
½ teacup double cream

3 Stir in the fish sauce, lemon juice and cream. Season, remembering that fish sauce is very salty. The lentils can be held at this stage and reheated later.

15g/¾oz fresh coriander,
chopped

4 When you're ready to serve, add the coriander, cook until wilted and serve immediately.

ROASTED CAULIFLOWER WITH TAHINI DRESSING

Roasting the cauliflower adds a different dimension and cutting it through its core makes an interesting visual slant. The tahini dressing is an added bonus but remember that all tahini pastes differ so you may need to adjust the amount used.

Utensils Large baking tray and mixing bowl

A little olive oil

1 Preheat the oven to 200°C/400°F/Gas 6. Pour a little olive oil onto the baking tray and heat in the oven.

1 large cauliflower
Salt and freshly ground black pepper

2 Cut the cauliflower in half and then into about 6 segments, cutting through the core which holds each segment together. Lay each piece flat on the now hot baking tray to brown well. Season and roast for 10 minutes, carefully turning halfway through the cooking time.

4 tablespoons tahini paste
2 small lemons, juiced
1 clove garlic
About ½ to 1 teacup water
15g/¾oz flat leaf parsley, chopped

3 In a bowl, mix together the tahini paste, lemon juice and garlic, gradually adding the water to make a dressing the consistency of double cream. Season and add the parsley.

4 To serve, pile the cauliflower into a hot serving dish. The cauliflower should be a good crispy brown but still have a bite to it. Drizzle the dressing over the top and serve immediately.

BASMATI RICE

Louise is constantly being asked about rice and how it's cooked. This recipe has been included as basmati is quick to cook and if you follow the instructions below, you simply cannot fail.

Utensils Strainer and large saucepan

225g/8oz basmati rice
Salt

1 Rinse the rice in a strainer and place in a large saucepan. Cover with boiling water, about 2½cm/1in above the rice level. Add salt and simmer for 10 minutes. Strain and place back in the same pan. Cover with a tight-fitting lid and leave to steam for 5–10 minutes off the heat.

2 To serve, gently fork through to separate the grains. (Each grain should still have its shape but will be just cooked.)

Top Man Tip Once the lid goes on the rice, it can be kept for up to approximately ½ hour. Always ensure that the rice is kept at a temperature of 65°C/149°F before eating. Any leftover rice should be thrown away and not reheated as bacteria can develop.

PESTO MASH

Utensils Large saucepan and a masher or ricer

900g/2lb Maris Piper or White potatoes
Salt

1 Peel and, if large, halve the potatoes and place them in a large saucepan of cold, salted water. Boil for 20–25 minutes.

1 teacup full fat milk
A large knob of butter
3 tablespoons double cream
2 heaped tablespoons fresh pesto
Salt and freshly ground black pepper

2 When the potatoes are soft (test with a sharp knife), drain and put them back into the pan. Leave to steam for a couple of seconds. Mash well, then add the milk, butter, cream, pesto and seasoning, and mash until all lumps have been removed.

3 Cover the saucepan with a lid or clingfilm if you want to keep the mash warm for a while.

CHAMP

Utensils Large and small saucepans, and a masher or ricer

900g/2lb Maris Piper
or White potatoes

1 Peel and halve the potatoes and place them in a large saucepan of cold, salted water. Bring to the boil and simmer for 20–25 minutes.

1 bunch spring onions
1 teacup full fat milk
3 tablespoons double cream
25g/1oz butter

2 Meanwhile, slice the spring onions and put them, together with the rest of the ingredients, into a small saucepan. Heat gently over a low heat until the butter has melted. Turn off the heat and leave to infuse.

Salt and freshly ground black
pepper

3 When the potatoes are soft (test them with a sharp knife), drain and put them back into the pan. Leave to steam for a couple of seconds. Mash the potatoes well and strain in the melted ingredients, reserving the spring onions. Season and continue to mash until all the lumps have been removed. Stir in the spring onions and season again.

4 Serve straight away, or this dish will keep warm in a saucepan with the lid on or covered in clingfilm for a few minutes.

PARSLEY MASH

Utensils Medium sized saucepan and a masher or ricer

900g/2lb Maris Piper
or White potatoes

1 Peel the potatoes, cut them in half if large and place in a medium saucepan. Cover with cold, salted water and boil for 20–25 minutes. Chop the parsley roughly.

1 teacup full fat milk
A large knob of butter
3 tablespoons double cream
Salt and freshly ground black
pepper
30g/1¼oz flat leaf parsley

2 When the potatoes are soft (test with a sharp knife), drain them. Put them back into the pan and leave to steam for a couple of seconds. Mash well, then add the butter and cream. Continue to mash until all lumps have been removed. Season, then add the chopped parsley and stir well.

3 This is great with plain roasted fish or something rich. It can be kept warm for a while in the saucepan, covered with a lid or clingfilm.

PUREED FENNEL

Utensils Large and small saucepans and a hand blender or food processor

3 fennel bulbs
A knob of butter
5 tablespoons water
1 lemon, juiced
Salt and freshly ground black pepper

1 Cut the fennel in half and slice it thinly. Melt the butter in the saucepan, add the water, lemon juice and seasoning. Bring to a simmer and cover with a lid. Cook on a low heat for 15–20 minutes or until very soft.

2 Pour the cooked fennel into a deep-sided container and use a hand blender or food processor to blend it to a smooth purée.

3 Reheat the fennel if necessary in a small pan.

BOULANGERE POTATOES

This can be cooked underneath the Marinaded/Grilled Roast Lamb on page 69, as the juices drip into the potatoes, adding extra flavour.

Utensils 24cm/9½in ovenproof dish

1.35kg/3lb Maris Piper or Red Desiree potatoes
1 large onion
2 cloves of garlic
2 sprigs of rosemary

1 Preheat the oven to 200°C/400°F/Gas 6. Peel and thinly slice the potatoes and onion. Crush the garlic, chop the rosemary and mix them with the onion.

Salt and freshly ground black pepper

2 Layer the potato slices in an ovenproof dish and top with the mix of onion, rosemary and garlic. Keep layering in this way until you have used up the potatoes and onion mix, seasoning each layer as you go. Finish with a layer of potato.

1 litre/1¾ pints vegetable stock
A little olive oil
Small knobs of butter
Chopped parsley, to garnish

3 Pour in the stock, drizzle with oil and dot with butter. Bake for 45 minutes until golden brown. Serve hot, garnished with chopped parsley.

SAUTEED MUSHROOMS AND ASPARAGUS

Utensils Large saucepan, tongs and large frying pan

24 large asparagus spears

1 Remove the tough stalk ends from the asparagus and cut into 5cm/2in lengths. Throw into a large saucepan of boiling salted water over a medium heat and cook for 30 seconds. Remove with tongs and immerse immediately in cold water.

450g/1lb oyster and shiitake mushrooms
A knob of butter
Salt and freshly ground black pepper

2 Cut the oyster mushrooms into large pieces and slice the shiitake. Melt a knob of butter in a large frying pan over a high heat. When foaming, add the mushrooms followed by the asparagus. Season well and stir fry for a couple of minutes, then serve immediately.

Top Man Tip Don't be tempted to buy an asparagus steamer – they are a waste of money. Asparagus is in season from May–June.

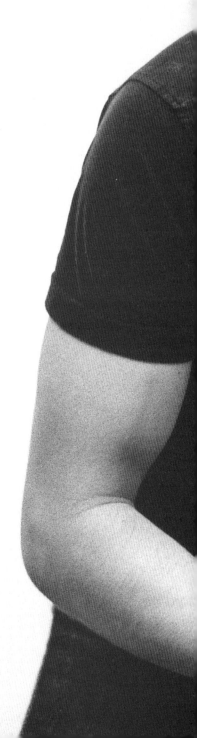

chapter eleven
chop, stock and two smokin' sausages

There is something especially appealing

about cooking your food over hot smouldering charcoal on a warm, summer evening. Is it cooking in the great outdoors or the sound of food sizzling on the grill? Is it the mouthwatering smoky aroma that fills the air, or is it that you can always hand over the sacred tongs to a willing guest while you enjoy an ice-cold beer?

Gone are the days when barbecues meant supermarket burgers and fatty sausages disintegrating on the grill. Chops, steaks and burgers are all delicious grilled but why not be more adventurous with what accompanies them? An interesting salad, an unusual marinade or a fresh salsa will add a little extra something to a standard grill and will take your barbecue to another level.

TABBOULEH

There are many variations of this quick, Middle Eastern salad. The key to an authentically refreshing Tabbouleh is to have plenty of fresh parsley and mint. It's perfect for a hot summer's day.

Utensils Large heatproof bowl

2 teacups bulgar (cracked) instant wheat

2–3 spring onions
4 medium plum or vine tomatoes, skin on
4 tablespoons olive oil
1 large lemon, juiced

A large bunch of flat leaf parsley
A large bunch of mint
Salt and freshly ground black pepper

1   Put the wheat into a large bowl, cover with boiling water and leave for 30 minutes.

2   Meanwhile slice the spring onions into ½cm/¼in slices and the tomatoes into 1cm/½in cubes. Drain the water from the wheat and place in a large bowl, together with the tomatoes and spring onions, olive oil and the juice from the lemon.

3   Roughly chop the parsley and mint. Add it to the tabbouleh mixture with plenty of seasoning and mix well.

4   This salad should be left to stand, covered, for about ½ hour in the fridge so that the flavours infuse. Don't leave it for any longer or it will become soggy. Tabbouleh should always be served chilled.

CAESAR SALAD

This is a popular salad dish that is very simple to make. There are many different variations for this classic salad and once you've tried our dressing, you won't go back to buying the bottled ones.

Utensils Baking tray, mixing bowl, grater and a large bowl or shallow serving dish

1 Preheat the oven to 200°C/400°F/Gas 6.

About 4 tablespoons of olive oil
50g/2oz bread chunks, torn
from small crusty white loaf
(each chunk should be
about 4cm/1½in)

2 To make the croutons, pour the oil onto a baking tray and roll the bread chunks in it. Bake in the oven for 10 minutes, remove and leave to cool.

275ml/½ pint good quality
mayonnaise
½ lemon, juiced
1 large clove of garlic, crushed

3 For the dressing, mix together the mayonnaise, lemon juice and garlic in a mixing bowl. If necessary, add a little cold water to dilute the dressing to the consistency of double cream.

6 Little Gem lettuces

4 Cut the core away from the bottom of the lettuces and the leaves will automatically come away. Wash and dry them carefully.

175g/6oz Parmigiano Reggiano
cheese
Salt and freshly ground black
pepper

5 Grate the cheese and add just over half of it to the dressing, reserving the rest for sprinkling, then season.

To Serve:
15g/¾oz fresh chives, chopped

6 Into a large bowl or shallow serving dish place a layer of lettuce leaves, drizzle with the dressing, sprinkle with some cheese and season. Repeat until all the leaves have been used. Drizzle the top layer with dressing, throw on the croutons, top with chopped chives and the remaining cheese.

LAMB BROCHETTES

Everyone loves a kebab! This version is slightly more sophisticated than the ones you may end up with on a Friday night. You can prepare them in advance and even leave them to marinate overnight in the fridge. Use either metal or wooden skewers, but soak the wooden variety in water first before they go on the barbecue to prevent them from burning.

Utensils Plastic or glass mixing bowl, 4 skewers (wooden or metal) and a small baking tray or grill pan

700g/1½lb lamb (leg steaks or chump chops), bone removed

1 Cut the lamb into 4cm/1½in cubes, removing the fat if necessary.

1 clove of garlic
15g/¾oz fresh rosemary leaves
7 tablespoons olive oil
Salt and freshly ground black pepper

2 Chop the garlic and remove the rosemary leaves from the stalks; chop roughly. Mix the garlic, rosemary and olive oil together in a bowl and add the meat, making sure it is completely covered with the marinade, then season.

3 Leave the kebabs to marinate, covered, in the fridge for as long as possible, preferably at least 4 hours.

4 Push the meat onto skewers, removing any excess oil. Season with salt and pepper and grill for 5–6 minutes each side on a barbecue, a baking tray or in a grill pan.

To Serve:
Hot chilli jam, chilli flavoured oil or Cucumber Raita (page 39), if liked

5 These brochettes are delicious served with hot chilli jam or chilli flavoured oil, which can be found in specialist sections of supermarkets. You could also serve them with Cucumber Raita.

Top Man Tip If you want something a little more substantial, serve the brochettes on a bed of Courgette Risotto (page 18), drizzled with basil oil or pesto dressing (whisk a little fresh pesto into prepared vinaigrette).

SPICED AUBERGINE SALAD

This simple, spicy and delicate salad is a variation on a classic Middle Eastern salad known as Iman Bayildi. The combination of spices with the aubergine gives it an exquisite taste that is hard to beat. As with most spicy dishes, it's better to use whole seeds and grind them yourself if possible as this gives a far superior flavour. Nevertheless if you don't have a pestle and mortar or a coffee grinder, try using preground or powdered coriander and cumin. Don't worry about salting the aubergines: it's really not necessary nowadays as the varieties produced are not bitter.

Utensils Medium saucepan and coffee grinder or pestle and mortar (optional)

2 medium aubergines
1 onion
A little olive oil

1 Dice the aubergines into 1cm/½in cubes, chop the onion and fry gently together in a saucepan with the oil over a low heat for 3 minutes or until soft.

2 teaspoons coriander seeds (or preground)
2 teaspoons cumin seeds (or preground)
¼ teaspoon turmeric

2 If using seeds, grind the coriander and cumin. Stir into the vegetables in the pan, together with the turmeric.

4 medium plum tomatoes
1 teacup currants
2 tablespoons red wine vinegar
Salt and freshly ground black pepper

3 Chop the tomatoes roughly into 1cm/½in squares and add to the pan with the currants and red wine vinegar. Season and cook gently for about 20 minutes or until the aubergine is soft.

30g/1¼oz mint
15g/¾oz flat leaf parsley

4 Roughly chop the mint and parsley. When the aubergine is cooked, take off the heat and stir in the parsley and mint; season.

Top Man Tip This salad should be served at room temperature, so leave it to cool before piling it onto a serving dish.

REAL AMERICAN HAMBURGERS WITH BLUE CHEESE

Serves 4
Preparation and Cooking Time:
15–20 minutes

After eating these, you'll never go back to processed packaged burgers.

Utensils Large bowl, barbecue or griddle pan

Salt and freshly ground black pepper
900g/2lb minced beef, with flecks of fat

1 Season and mix the meat well in a large bowl. Divide into four and mould firmly into rounds roughly 9cm/3½in round and 2cm/¾in thick.

2 Grill the burgers on a hot barbecue or griddle pan or place under the grill for 5 minutes on each side for rare or 8 minutes on each side for medium.

Blue cheese or Cheddar/Swiss cheese (if preferred), to taste

3 Blue cheese can be melted on top of the burgers for 3-4 minutes before serving, or you could try Cheddar or Swiss cheese.

To Serve:
4 toasted soft baps
Assorted fillings such as rocket leaves, sliced spring onions, thinly sliced beef tomatoes and pickled cucumbers; mayonnaise, any relishes, tomato ketchup and mustard,
also Oven Roasted Chips (page 94)

4 Serve with toasted soft baps, assorted fillings and Oven Roasted Chips (see page 94).

Top Man Tip When entertaining or trying to impress children, you cannot go wrong with these burgers. Everyone loves picking their own fillings and generally making a mess. Throw some woody herbs, such as rosemary or thyme, onto the coals to add extra flavour. The aroma is delicious.

Serves 4

Preparation and Cooking Time:

10 minutes plus 4 hours

for marinading

CHICKEN BROCHETTES

Utensils Zester, large bowl, 4 wooden or metal skewers, a small baking tray or grill pan

8 chicken thighs, boned
and skinned

1   Cut each chicken thigh into quarters.

1 medium lemon
8 tablespoons olive oil
1 teaspoon paprika or smoked
paprika or ½ teaspoon cayenne
Salt and freshly ground pepper

2   Remove the zest and squeeze the juice from the lemon; mix with the oil and paprika or cayenne in a large bowl. Add the meat, season and stir well. Cover and leave to marinate in the fridge for as long as you can, preferably at least 4 hours.

3   Push the meat onto skewers, scraping off any excess oil. Season and grill for 4 minutes on each side.

To Serve:

Tabbouleh (page 127), fresh
salsa (page 23) or Cucumber
Raita (page 39)

4   Serve with Tabbouleh and fresh salsa or Cucumber Raita. These can all be made in advance.

Serves 4

Preparation and Cooking time:

35–40 minutes

PORK RIBS WITH PLUM SAUCE

Utensils Medium and large saucepans, pastry brush

1   Separate the ribs with a sharp knife, then bring a large pan of salted water to the boil. Add the ribs and cook for 5 minutes; drain.

900g/2lb pork spare ribs

2   Heat the oils together in a pan, add the garlic and ginger, and cook gently for 1–2 minutes. Stir in the plum sauce, sherry, hoisin and soy sauces; heat gently.

2 tablespoons sunflower oil
1 teaspoon sesame oil
2 garlic cloves, crushed
2½cm/1in piece of fresh ginger,
grated
⅔ teacup plum sauce
2 tablespoons dry sherry
2 tablespoons hoisin sauce
2 tablespoons soy sauce

3   Brush the sauce over the ribs and grill on a cool part of the barbecue for 20 minutes.

PESTO BREAD

This simple and quick to make bread is great served with barbecued food. Pesto combines well with fresh, crusty white bread and the result is delicious. Serve the bread as either an accompaniment or as an appetiser on its own.

Utensils Mixing bowl, teaspoon or palette knife and roll of kitchen foil

1 Preheat the oven to 200°C/400°F/Gas 6.

1 small baguette
or whole ciabatta bread

2 Slice the bread on the diagonal without cutting all the way through and place it on a very large piece of foil.

1 tub (125g/5oz) fresh pesto
Salt and freshly ground black pepper
2 tablespoons olive oil

3 In a bowl, season the pesto and mix in the olive oil. Using a teaspoon or palette knife, spread the pesto mix onto the bread in between the incisions. Wrap well in the foil and bake in the oven for 15 minutes.

Top Man Tip Open the foil for the last few minutes of cooking so that the bread becomes crisp.

GARLIC BREAD

Utensils Mixing bowl and kitchen foil

1 medium baguette or whole ciabatta
1 clove of garlic
15g/¾oz fresh flat leaf parsley
50g/2oz butter, at room temperature
Salt and freshly ground black pepper

1 Preheat the oven to 200°C/400°F/Gas 6. Slice through the bread on the diagonal without cutting it all the way through. Place on a large piece of foil big enough to wrap around the bread. Chop the garlic and the parsley. Mix with the butter, season and spread onto the bread, pushing it through the incisions.

2 Wrap the bread tightly in the foil and bake for 15 minutes (open up the foil to allow the bread to crispen up for the last few minutes). Serve hot.

Top Man Tip Other fresh chopped herbs can be added to your taste.

COURGETTE AND MINT SALAD

Serves 4
Preparation Time: 5 minutes

This Italian salad is probably the easiest in the world! It has the added bonus that you can make it beforehand and leave it in the fridge until needed.

Utensils Small mandolin (see Top Man Tip) and large serving dish with tall sides

15g/¾oz mint

450g/1lb courgettes
Salt and freshly ground black pepper
1 medium lemon
Olive oil

1   Remove the mint leaves from the stalks and roughly chop them.

2   Slice the ends away from the courgettes, then slice them lengthways as thinly as possible. Place a layer in the bottom of a serving dish. Season and sprinkle with some of the mint, a good squeeze of lemon and drizzle with olive oil. Repeat in this way until all the ingredients have been used up.

3   Cover and leave to marinate in the fridge for as long as possible, preferably 1 hour. Serve chilled.

Top Man Tip It is very useful to have in your equipment cupboard a small plastic or metal mandolin. This is an inexpensive specialist cutting instrument which will slice efficiently on one width. A mandolin would be the perfect tool for slicing the courgettes.

ROASTED POTATOES WITH SAGE AND ROSEMARY

Serves 4
Preparation and Cooking Time:
20–25 minutes

These are a simple, crispy and tasty alternative to roast potatoes.

Utensils Large saucepan, baking tray, colander, serving dish and kitchen paper

900g/2lb Red Desiree or White potatoes

1 Trim the sides away from each potato to create cubes – all the peel should be removed. Cut into 2cm/¾in slices and then again into smaller cubes. Fill a large saucepan with cold, salted water and bring to the boil over a medium heat. Preheat the oven to 200°C/400°F/Gas 6.

3 sprigs of rosemary
About 8 small sage leaves
Olive oil for drizzling

2 Roughly chop the herbs. Pour a little oil into the baking tray. When the water starts to boil rapidly, drain the potatoes into a colander and shake them to remove excess water.

Salt and freshly ground black pepper
1 clove of garlic

3 Turn the potatoes out onto the heated baking tray, season well and roast for 15 minutes. Chop the garlic and stir it into the potatoes along with the herbs. Roast for a further 5 minutes.

To Serve:
Extra salt

4 Scoop the potatoes into a warmed serving dish lined with kitchen paper. Pull away the paper and serve with some extra salt.

TARRAGON INFUSED SEA BASS

Serves 4
Preparation and Cooking Time:
10 minutes

Fish cooks wonderfully well on the barbecue. Cooking it on a bed of tarragon allows the flavours of the herb to be gently released into the fish. This is quite an unusual method of cooking but it is absolutely delicious.

Utensils Grill, griddle or frying pan, pastry brush and fish slice or palette knife

Olive oil
Salt and freshly ground black pepper
4 x 175g/6oz fillets of sea bass or any other firm fish such as halibut, red mullet or turbot

1 Heat the grill, griddle or frying pan to a medium heat. When hot, brush with oil. Season the fish and place it skin side down. Cook for 3 minutes.

A few bunches of fresh tarragon

2 Divide the tarragon into four and press a thick layer of herbs firmly onto the fish, stalks and all. With a fish slice or palette knife, carefully turn the fish and cook it, with the tarragon underneath, for another 3 minutes to allow the flavours to infuse. Season again.

To Serve:
1 lemon, cut into quarters and extra virgin olive oil

3 Serve on hot plates with lemon quarters and a drizzle of extra virgin olive oil, along with the now charred tarragon leaves.

Top Man Tip Try other herbs for different flavours.

GRILLED JAMAICAN TILAPIA WITH AVOCADO SALSA

Serves 4

Preparation and Cooking Time:
25-30 minutes

It is very easy to serve a large whole fish when barbecuing for a few people. Jamaican tilapia is good for barbecues and readily available in most supermarkets. If you use a very large fish, adjust the cooking time accordingly.

Utensils Pastry brush, mixing bowl and a hinged grilling basket

900g/2lb whole Jamaican tilapia or snapper or sea bass, descaled
A little olive oil
Salt and freshly ground black pepper

1 With a sharp knife, slash the main body of the fish a few times so that the heat will penetrate well through the flesh. Brush with olive oil and season.

2 avocados
1 red onion
2 limes, juiced
15g/¾oz mint, chopped

2 To make the salsa, halve the avocados and remove the stones. Cut iinto long, thin slices lengthways and then into small cubes. Cut the onion to the same size. Mix together in a bowl with the lime juice and chopped mint; season. Cover and chill until needed.

3 When the grill or coals are smoulderingly hot but not flaming, place the fish in a hinged grilling basket. Grill for 5–10 minutes on each side until opaque and firm.

To Serve:
Chilled salsa, a tomato and basil or green salad and crusty bread

4 Carefully remove the flesh from the fish bones and serve on warmed plates with a spoonful of chilled salsa. Serve with a simple tomato and basil or green salad and plenty of crusty bread.

Top Man Tip When barbecuing, make sure that the coals are smouldering and never flaming otherwise you risk burning the food. Adjust the barbecue grill or tray as needed.

chapter twelve

have your cake and eat it

There's no need to panic

at the thought of making dessert. Some people enjoy rich desserts, some prefer lighter variations and some strange people don't like them at all. The best way to tackle desserts is to have a repertoire of standard recipes that covers all occasions and hopefully we've provided that here.

When thinking about what to prepare, take into account what is seasonally available – nothing can beat the fresh fruits that are on offer in the summer months. Likewise it is also important to consider the weather – what could beat something warming and comforting for that particularly cold winter's night?

MARMALADE PUDDING

This is a great winter warmer and a recipe handed down from Louise's grandmother. Fresh breadcrumbs are essential and therefore a food processor is a necessity. This pudding can be made in advance and gently reheated in a low oven (170°C/325°F/Gas 3) for 25 minutes.

Utensils Food processor, large bowl, electric or hand whisk and 20cm/8in ovenproof dish

3 medium eggs
75g/3oz butter at room temperature
1½ tablespoons caster sugar

1 Preheat the oven to 190°C/375°F/Gas 5. Separate the egg yolks from the whites and reserve the whites. Using a whisk, whip the yolks, butter and sugar together in a bowl until light and pale.

3 tablespoons marmalade
150ml/¼ pint milk
60g/2½oz fresh white breadcrumbs, chopped in a food processor for a few seconds

2 Beat in the marmalade, milk and breadcrumbs.

3 Whisk the egg whites until firm. Beat ¼ of the whisked egg whites into the marmalade mixture and then carefully fold in the remainder.

4 Pour the mixture into an ovenproof dish and bake for 20-25 minutes.

To Serve:
Thick double cream

5 Serve warm with thick double cream.

CREAMY YOGHURT PUDDING

Serves 4

Preparation Time: 15 minutes

plus 1 hour in the fridge

Utensils Medium glass mixing bowl, hand whisk, plastic scraper and large serving bowl

275ml/½ pint double cream

1 Pour the cream into a bowl and whisk until semi-thick, about the same consistency as the yoghurt.

275ml/½ pint natural yoghurt (not the French set variety)

2 Using a plastic scraper, carefully fold the yoghurt into the cream.

250g/9oz fresh strawberries or any other soft fruit

3 Cut the stalks off the strawberries, then cut them in half and place in the base of a large serving bowl.

5 dessertspoons demerara sugar

4 Spoon a quarter of the yoghurt mixture onto the strawberries and sprinkle with a layer of sugar. Keep layering the cream and sugar until all the yoghurt mixture has been used. Finish with a layer of sugar.

5 Cover and leave in the fridge for about 1 hour so that the sugar dissolves into the creamy mixture.

6 To serve, spoon into individual serving bowls or layer the pudding into tall glasses.

CREME BRULEE

Utensils Hand whisk, large heat proof bowl, medium saucepan, 6 ramekins (7cm/2¾in base) and a roasting tin with sides

5 medium egg yolks
75g/3oz caster sugar

1 Whisk the egg yolks and 75g/3oz sugar into a large heatproof bowl until pale. Preheat the oven to 150°C/300°F/Gas 2.

225ml/8 fl oz full fat milk
225ml/8 fl oz double cream
1 vanilla pod or 1 teaspoon
vanilla essence

2 Measure the milk and cream out into a saucepan and bring to the boil over a medium heat. If you're using a vanilla pod, slit it in half and use the end of the knife to scrape out any seeds. Stir into the milk mixture, along with the pod shell.

3 When the milk is just about to boil, remove the pod and pour the milk onto the yolks, stirring continuously until the sugar has dissolved. If using vanilla essence, add this now. Pour the mixture into a jug and then into 6 ramekins.

4 Boil the kettle. Put the ramekins into a roasting tin and pour boiling water about halfway up the sides. Carefully move the tin into the oven and gently cook for 25 minutes. The custards should be just cooked, yet still slightly wobbly. As they cool, they will continue to set.

3 dessertspoons caster sugar

5 Set the grill to its highest setting and spoon 3 dessertspoons of sugar very thinly and evenly over the top of the custard. As it grills, it will start to bubble and then caramelise, but watch carefully as it will burn very easily. Leave to cool in the fridge.

To Serve:
Sieved icing sugar and cocoa
powder (optional)

6 The tops can be sprinkled with sieved icing sugar and cocoa powder to serve, if desired.

Top Man Tip Use the remaining whites to make meringue (page 151) for a Pavlova.

Serves 4
Preparation and Cooking Time:
20–25 minutes plus 1 hour
standing time for the batter

CREPES SUZETTES

This variation on the 70's favourite, which is enjoying a comeback, is very simple and easy to prepare in advance.

Utensils Small saucepan, food processor or whisk, mixing bowl, zester, crêpe pan or large non-stick frying pan and metal palette knife

Batter:
60g/2½oz butter, plus extra for frying
2 eggs
350ml/12 fl oz full fat milk
110g/4oz plain flour
Salt

1 To make the batter, melt the butter in a small saucepan. Put the eggs, milk, cooled melted butter, flour and salt into a food processor. Blend for a few minutes until smooth and leave to stand for 1 hour if possible. If you don't have a food processor, the batter can be made by putting the flour into a bowl, making a well in the middle and adding the rest of the ingredients. Gradually whisk the flour into the milk mixture.

Sauce:
5 large oranges
8 tablespoons caster sugar
4 tablespoons Grand Marnier

2 For the sauce, zest 3 oranges and put to one side. Juice all 5 oranges and put into the frying pan with the sugar. Start to simmer the mixture and add the Grand Marnier and orange zest. Simmer for 20 minutes or until thick. The sauce will hold at this stage.

3 To make the crêpes, melt a little butter in the frying pan. Pour any excess into a bowl. Over a high heat, add a ladleful of pancake batter and move the pan around to cover the base quickly. Wait for a few seconds and check to see if the underside is lightly browned. Turn over using a palette knife and cook for a further few seconds.

4 Leave the crêpes to cool on a plate, stacking up as you go. Don't worry about putting anything between each layer; it really isn't necessary. In general your first crêpe may not be very good. Don't worry, just eat it! The crêpes will hold at this stage. If wrapped well with clingfilm, both the pancakes and the sauce can be stored overnight in the fridge.

To Serve:
Cream or vanilla ice cream

5 Reheat the sauce in the frying pan. Fold each crêpe into quarters and immerse it in the sauce, spooning sauce over each crêpe as you go to reheat. Place 2 crêpes on each warmed plate with lots of the sauce spooned over. Serve with cream or vanilla ice cream.

COCONUT RICE PUDDING WITH CARAMELISED BANANA

Serves 4

Preparation and Cooking Time:
1 hour 35 minutes

Utensils Large saucepan, large ovenproof dish and large frying pan

1 Preheat the oven to 140°C/275°F/Gas 1.

60g/2½oz butter
75g/3oz caster sugar
1 litre/1 pint 570ml full fat milk
250ml/8 fl oz tin coconut milk
Pinch of salt
100g/3½oz round grain
pudding rice

2 Melt the butter in a large saucepan over a low heat and add the sugar, heating gently. Stir in the milk, coconut milk, salt and pudding rice; bring to the boil.

3 Transfer to an ovenproof dish and place in the oven for 1 hour, covered.

4 Just before the rice pudding is ready, peel and slice the bananas on the diagonal. Melt the butter in a large frying pan, add the sugar and stir until golden. Turn up the heat slightly and add the bananas. They will soon cook and caramelise.

4 bananas
Large knob of butter
3 tablespoons caster sugar

5 To serve, spoon a generous portion of rice into a bowl and top with the caramelised banana.

RASPBERRY ICED MERINGUE

This is a quick and light recipe that's perfect for summer entertaining. It's very important to combine the meringue and frozen yoghurt as quickly as possible and return it to a frozen temperature immediately. A recipe like this is probably the best way to use shop-bought, ready-made meringues.

Utensils Spring-form cake tin (15cm/6in), 1 large bowl, metal spoon, high-sided container, hand blender, sieve and small ladle

2 x 500ml/just under 1 pint tubs raspberry frozen yoghurt
2½ ready made meringue nests, broken into large chunks

Coulis:
250g/9oz frozen raspberries
A little icing sugar (optional)

To Serve:
Fresh mint sprigs and extra fresh raspberries

1 Line the cake tin completely with clingfilm. Scoop the frozen yoghurt into a large bowl and add the meringue. Using a metal spoon, roughly combine the two together quickly as you don't want the yoghurt to melt. Spoon the mixture into the cake tin and level out. Cover with more clingfilm and put the tin straight back into the freezer.

2 Defrost the raspberries, place in a high-sided container and use a hand blender to purée. Sieve the purée into a bowl using a scraper or the bowl of a small ladle to push it through. If needed, add a little icing sugar but bear in mind that the meringue is very sweet.

3 To serve, peel away the clingfilm, cut the meringue into slices and place on a plate. Spoon the coulis over one side of the meringue. Garnish with a sprig of mint and extra raspberries.

Top Man Tip At certain times of the year it is perfectly acceptable to use frozen raspberries – and they are cheaper than the yearly crop of summer raspberries – but only use them for a sauce or blended within a recipe. Obviously, in the summer when they are in abundance and full of flavour, fresh are far superior.

STICKY TOFFEE AND BANANA PUDDING

This is a gooey and delicious winter steamed pudding that everyone seems to like. Its flavour really benefits from the addition of bananas.

Utensils 8 metal dariole moulds or an 18cm/7in spring-form cake tin and greaseproof paper, large bowl, mixing bowl, hand whisk, metal skewer and small saucepan

Knob of butter for greasing
225g/8oz chopped dates
275ml/½ pint hot tea

1 Preheat the oven to 170°C/325°F/Gas 3. Wipe around the dariole moulds with the butter (if using a cake tin, cut a circle of greaseproof paper to line the bottom). In a bowl, soak the dates in the hot tea for 15 minutes.

110g/4oz butter, at room temperature
175g/6oz caster sugar
3 eggs

2 Using a hand whisk, cream together 110g/4oz butter and the sugar until pale. Beat in the eggs one at a time.

1 teaspoon bicarbonate of soda
1 teaspoon vanilla essence
225g/8oz self raising flour
3 bananas, mashed

3 Add the bicarbonate of soda and vanilla essence to the date and tea mixture. Carefully stir them in, together with the flour and mashed bananas.

4 Spoon into the moulds or tin and bake in the oven for 30 minutes in the darioles or 1 hour in the tin. The pudding is ready when a skewer inserted into the centre comes out clean.

Toffee Sauce:
50g/2oz butter
50g/2oz muscovado sugar
½ teacup double cream
50g/2oz pecans, chopped

5 To make the sauce, melt 50g/2oz butter in the saucepan, add the sugar and stir for 2–3 minutes. Add the cream and continue to stir until the sugar has dissolved, then add the pecans.

To Serve:
Whipped, double or clotted cream (optional)

6 To serve, reheat the sauce. Turn out the cooked pudding onto individual plates and top with hot sauce. Whipped, double or clotted cream can be served separately.

BITTER ORANGE SALAD WITH GRAND MARNIER ICE CREAM

Serves 4
Preparation Time: 10–15 minutes

This refreshing salad is a great stand-by pudding as it takes only minutes to make. It is also great to serve with any chocolate cake or dessert.

Utensils Serrated knife, chopping board, edged dish and small saucepan

4 oranges

1 Use a serrated knife to slice the ends off each orange, place on a board and cut away the sides, following the curved line of the fruit. Slice away the peel, making sure all the white pith is removed and cut horizontally into ½cm/¼in slices. Arrange in an edged dish.

Caramel:
150g/5oz caster sugar
10 tablespoons water

2 For the caramel, place the sugar and 4 tablespoons of water in a small saucepan over a medium heat. Stir and leave to boil. Measure out 6 tablespoons water and put to one side. Watch the caramel as it will take a while then change very quickly from golden to dark brown. When it starts to turn a medium/dark brown, carefully pour in the water – it will spit. Swirl the saucepan over the heat until the bubbles subside and an even, thick syrup is left. Leave to cool slightly and pour over the sliced oranges.

To Serve:
570ml/1 pint Grand Marnier ice cream and fresh mint

3 Serve with a good scoop of ice cream on top and add a sprig of fresh mint.

Top Man Tip If you cannot find Grand Marnier ice cream, substitute with vanilla and drizzle Grand Marnier liqueur over the top.

MARSALA BAKED PEARS

Whole baked fruit is a great way to cook as it encapsulates all the flavours and juices inside the fruit's own skin. Marsala, an Italian sweet wine, is a very versatile ingredient, which is handy to have in your larder.

Utensils Small saucepan and an ovenproof dish with lid

75ml/3 fl oz cold water
275g/10oz caster sugar
1 cinnamon stick or 1 teaspoon ground cinnamon
6 pears, rinsed, skin on
25g/1oz butter

1 Preheat the oven to 150°C/300°F/Gas 2. Pour the water into a small pan, add the sugar and stir once. Leave on a medium heat and gradually the sugar will caramelise. As the sugar is heating, break the cinnamon stick in half (if using) or add the ground cinnamon to the ovenproof dish with the pears and dot with butter.

175ml/6 fl oz Marsala

2 Let the caramel darken in the pan (this wll take approximately 15 minutes), but be warned that it quickly changes from dark brown to black. Add the Marsala carefully – it will spit. Lower the heat and swirl the sugar in the pan to produce a thick, even liquid. Pour the liquid over the pears and if you don't have a lid to the dish, cover it with foil. Bake for 1 hour.

To Serve:
Crème fraîche or thick double cream

3 Serve hot, with plenty of thick sauce, crème fraîche or thick double cream.

Top Man Tip A sweet dessert wine could be used as an alternative if Marsala is not available.

CHOCOLATE FONDANT PUDDINGS

Serves 4

Preparation and cooking time:

45 minutes

These very rich, deluxe chocolate puddings are simply divine. No chocolate lover will be able to resist them, guaranteed! When cooked, the chocolate 'ganache' becomes meltingly soft in between the crisp cake coating. The quality of chocolate depends to a large extent on the price you pay. You cannot make a good chocolate dish with inferior chocolate. By rule of thumb it is best to aim for around 60–70% cocoa solids. See page 159 for mail order details if it is very difficult for you to buy good chocolate locally.

Utensils 2 small Pyrex bowls, small saucepan, mixing bowl, whisk, plastic scrapers, 4 ramekins (7cm/2¾in) and a baking tray

40g/1½oz good quality chocolate
7 tablespoons double cream

1 Break 40g/1½oz chocolate into small pieces. Put it into a Pyrex bowl which fits over a saucepan a quarter filled with water (the water should not touch the bowl) over a medium heat. When the chocolate has melted, pour in the double cream; stir well and it will change into a thick, semi-solid mixture known as 'ganache', which is used as the base for truffles. Cover and chill.

90g/3½oz chocolate, at least 65% cocoa butter
75g/3oz unsalted butter

2 Break 90g/3½oz chocolate into a bowl with the butter and place over a medium heat until melted. Take off the heat.

3 Preheat the oven 180°C/350°F/Gas 4.

2 medium eggs
50g/2oz caster sugar
2 tablespoons cocoa powder

4 In a mixing bowl, separate the eggs and whisk the whites until soft peaks form. Stir the sugar, cocoa and yolks into the second mix of chocolate, then mix in a quarter of the egg whites. Fold in the rest carefully using a plastic scraper, turning the bowl gently as you go.

5 To make three layers, use a dessertspoon to place a spoonful of the egg and chocolate mixture in the base of each ramekin. Take a small teaspoon of the now hard ganache and place on top. Cover with another layer of the first chocolate mixture and smooth to an even level. Place on a baking tray and bake in the oven for 12 minutes.

To Serve:
Vanilla ice cream

6 Serve hot with a separate scoop of vanilla ice cream. These little puddings can be made in advance and cooked when needed.

PAVLOVA

This is a simple and light classic dessert. A Pavlova has the addition of cornflour and vinegar to give it a delicately crisp outer coating, perfectly complemented by the soft, squidgy interior which resembles a marshmallow. This particular version was created by Victoria Blashford-Snell of the wonderful *Books for Cooks*. Pavlovas are just as good in winter as summer, depending on the topping available at the time.

Utensils Large baking tray, baking parchment or greaseproof paper, large bowl, electric whisk and palette knife

6 medium egg whites
350g/12oz caster sugar

1 Preheat the oven to 180°C/350°F/Gas 4. Line the baking tray with baking parchment or greaseproof paper. Whisk the egg whites in a large bowl until white and quite firm. Then whisk in the sugar, 1 tablespoon at a time, until the meringue becomes very thick and glossy in texture.

2 teaspoons cornflour
1 teaspoon vinegar

2 Whisk in the cornflour and vinegar. Spoon onto the paper using a palette knife and shape into a circle with a slightly dipped centre. Bake for 5 minutes then turn down the heat to 140°C/275°F/Gas 1 and bake for a further 1¼ hours.

Filling:
250ml/8 fl oz double cream

3 Leave to cool on the paper, then carefully peel the paper away and place the meringue on a large serving dish. Whip the cream until just thick. If the meringue is at all damaged, use the cream as a cover-up.

Topping:
Either: Berries, bananas, lemon curd, chocolate, ice cream, strawberries or yoghurt

4 Pile high with your chosen topping and serve.

Top Man Tip This can be served with a coulis (see Raspberry Iced Meringue, page 146).

PANETTONE BREAD AND BUTTER PUDDING

Although we have two bread and butter puddings in this section, they are very different and it was too difficult for us to choose between them as they are both so good! Panettone, a traditional Italian enriched bread, can be found all year round in good Italian delis and at Christmas time in most supermarkets.

Utensils Large saucepan, electric whisk, large mixing bowl, large ovenproof dish (about 5cm/2in deep), large sieve and a roasting tin

570ml/1 pint full fat milk
570ml/1 pint double cream
1 vanilla pod
or 2 teaspoons vanilla essence

1 To make the custard base, bring the milk and cream just to a boil in a saucepan and take off the heat. Cut the vanilla pod in half (if using) and with a sharp knife, scrape out the seeds and add both to the pan.

4 medium eggs
175g/6oz caster sugar

2 In a bowl, whisk the eggs with the sugar until slightly pale. Whisk the milk and cream, remove the pod shell and whisk together with the eggs. If using vanilla essence, add now.

2 thick slices panettone
3 tablespoons cognac

3 Preheat the oven to 170°C/325°F/Gas 3. Place the panettone slices in the ovenproof dish, drizzling cognac between each layer. Ladle the custard through a sieve and leave the panettone to soak for at least 15 minutes or longer.

4 Place the dish in a roasting tin and half fill with hot water. Bake for about 45 minutes. When cooked the pudding will have a slight crust on top, but will still be slightly wobbly inside.

To Serve:
Fresh berries

5 Serve either hot or cold with fresh berries.

Top Man Tip If a vanilla pod is not available, try vanilla essence although the flavour is not quite as good.

MICHAEL CAINE'S BREAD AND BUTTER PUDDING

Serves 4–6

Preparation and Cooking Time:
1 hour plus 1 hour resting

Michael Caine gave us his favourite version of this English classic. The addition of bananas and rum is a welcome and delicious change.

Utensils Ovenproof dish and mixing bowl

1   Preheat the oven to 150°C/300°F/Gas 2.

2   Prepare an ovenproof dish by greasing it with butter. Butter several slices of bread and place in layers between the sliced bananas and sultanas.

Large knob of butter
10 slices of medium sliced
white bread, crusts removed
2 bananas, sliced
50g/2oz sultanas

3   Beat the eggs in with the sugar and add the milk. Then add the vanilla essence and rum.

3 eggs
4 tablespoons sugar
570ml/1 pint full fat milk
4 drops of vanilla essence
2 generous tablespoons rum

4   Pour the mixture over the bread and butter and leave it, covered with clingfilm or foil, for 1 hour in the fridge. Bake, uncovered, for 45 minutes.

5   Serve in warmed bowls with double cream or good-quality vanilla ice cream – yum!

To Serve:
Double cream or good quality
vanilla ice cream

Top Man Tip Use the paper that the butter came in to grease the ovenproof dish.

APPLE AND AMARETTI STRUDEL

Utensils Mixing bowl, pestle and mortar or rolling pin, small saucepan, pastry brush and a large baking sheet

3 small Bramley apples
2½ tablespoons soft brown sugar
12 amaretti biscuits
3 tablespoons sultanas

1 Preheat the oven to 180°C/350°F/Gas 4. Peel the apples and cut them into quarters. Remove the core section with a sharp knife, slice thinly and mix with the sugar and the sultanas. Crush the amaretti biscuits with a pestle and mortar or put them in a bag and crush them with a heavy object such as a rolling pin.

75g/3oz butter
5 large sheets of filo pastry

2 Melt the butter in a small saucepan and take off the heat. Lay one sheet of filo flat, keeping the rest covered with a damp tea towel. Brush well with melted butter and sprinkle with some of the crushed amaretti biscuits. Lay another sheet over this, half overlapping the undersheet, and repeat this procedure until the last sheet, which lays central.

3 Line a large baking sheet with foil and place the sheets on top. Pile the apples into the centre and roll, keeping the seam underneath and tuck in the ends. Brush generously with butter and bake for 25–30 minutes.

To Serve:
Icing sugar and thick cream

4 To serve, cut into thick slices and serve hot sprinkled with icing sugar. Serve with a large spoon of thick cream on the side.

Serves 4

Preparation and Cooking Time:

50–55 minutes

LEMON PUDDING

Utensils Electric or hand whisk, 18cm/7in ovenproof dish, 2 mixing bowls, roasting tin, zester and grater

100g/3½oz butter at room temperature, plus a little extra for greasing
175g/6oz caster sugar

1 Preheat the oven to 180°C/350°F/Gas 4. For this recipe it is probably easiest to prepare all the ingredients before starting. Using the electric hand whisk or whisk, cream the butter and the sugar in a large bowl until fluffy and white.

4 lemons, zest and juice
4 medium eggs, separated
50g/2oz plain flour
110ml/4 fl oz full fat milk

2 Beat in the lemon zest and juice, beat in the egg yolks, one at a time, and then the flour and milk. The mixture may look slightly curdled but don't worry.

3 Whisk the whites in a separate bowl until firm and fold gently into the mixture. Pour into the dish, place in a deep roasting tin and pour hot water halfway up the side of the dish. This method helps to cook the pudding gently and it's known as a 'bain-marie'. Bake in the oven for about 45 minutes until the top is golden brown and has risen.

4 Serve the pudding hot. As you cut through the sponge you'll find a creamy, lemony sauce.

Serves 4

Preparation and Cooking Time:

10–12 minutes

APPLES IN A CARDAMOM FUDGE SAUCE

Apples are at their best in the autumn. The cardamom in this fudge sauce gives an interesting twist.

Utensils Large frying pan

900g/2lb Granny Smith apples
110g/4oz butter
175g/6oz light brown sugar
2 teaspoons ground cardamom
150ml/¼ pint orange juice

1 Peel and core the apples. Cut into quarters and thickly slice. Melt the butter in a large frying pan over a low heat and stir in the sugar. When the butter has melted, add the cardamom and orange juice. Boil for 3 minutes.

To Serve:
A mixture of half yoghurt, half thick cream

2 Turn the heat up and cook the apples for 3–5 minutes or until soft. Serve with a mixture of half yoghurt and half thick cream, mixed together. The apples can be reheated very gently on a low heat.

PANNA COTTA

This is a traditional Italian dessert made with undeniably indulgent thick double cream. It's not great for the waistline, but seeing as it's so delicious, who cares? This is very popular in Italy and it's becoming increasingly fashionable over here too.

Utensils Large and small saucepans, mixing bowl, hand whisk and 6 ramekins (7.5cm/3in base)

570ml/1 pint double cream
1 vanilla pod
Peel from 1½ lemons

1 Pour 450ml/¾ pint of the cream into a large saucepan. To add more of an intense vanilla flavour, cut the vanilla pod in half, scrape out the soft seeds inside and add to the pan with its outer casing. Add the lemon peel and simmer for 5 minutes or until the mixture has reduced by one third. Remove the cooked lemon peel and keep to one side.

60ml/2½ fl oz cold milk
2 teaspoons gelatine

2 In a small saucepan, heat the milk to boiling point. Take off the heat and stir in the gelatine; it should dissolve quite quickly. Pour this into the hot cream mixture, sieve and leave to cool slightly.

60g/2½oz icing sugar
55ml/2 fl oz grappa

3 In a bowl, whip the remaining cream with the icing sugar until semi-firm, fold it into the cooled cream and add the grappa.

4 Put a piece of reserved lemon zest into each of the 6 ramekins and fill with the stirred cream mixture. Cover and leave to set in the fridge for at least 2 hours.

To Serve:
1 punnet of raspberries and
extra grappa

5 Turn out onto plates and serve with fresh raspberries and extra grappa drizzled over the top. If you're nervous about the turning out, serve in their ramekins.

Top Man Tip As an alternative, you could serve this in a small coffee cup topped with hot expresso. Or in the summer, leave in a small dish or glass and top with Summer Pudding mixture (page 153).

STRAWBERRY SOUFFLE

Don't despair when you read that often-dreaded word – soufflé! They really are not anything to be nervous about. As long as you organise your ingredients beforehand, the finishing and actual cooking only take a few minutes. Any fruit purée can be substituted for the strawberry used here.

Utensils 4 ramekins (7.5cm/3in), pastry brush, 1 small saucepan, 1 heatproof bowl, blender (optional), whisk, baking tray and small sieve

25g/1oz butter, softened to room temperature
25g/1oz caster sugar

1 First prepare your ramekins by brushing the insides well with softened butter; be sure to brush right up to the top. The layer should be quite thick as it helps the soufflé to rise. Sprinkle inside each dish with caster sugar and roll the ramekins around so that the sugar sticks.

Custard:
175ml/6 fl oz milk
2 medium egg yolks
15g/¾oz caster sugar
2½ teaspoons cornflour

2 In a saucepan heat the milk. Separate the eggs in a small bowl, saving the whites to whisk later. Beat the egg yolks and sugar together, then whisk in the cornflour. Pour on the now-hot milk and pour back into the pan.

3 Place the pan over a low heat and continue to whisk the custard until thick and smooth; this will only take a few minutes. Pour into a clean bowl and cover with clingfilm. This should touch the custard or a skin will form. At this stage weigh out the ingredients for the meringue and strawberries, but don't go any further until you're ready to eat.

Meringue:
3 medium egg whites
40g/1½oz caster sugar

4 Preheat the oven to 200°C/400°F/Gas 6 and place a baking tray in the oven to heat through. Whisk the egg whites until white and stiff, then gradually add the sugar and beat again until firm and glossy (this will only take a few minutes).

175g/6oz strawberries

5 After removing the stalks, mash the strawberries with a fork or blend to a smooth purée and stir into the now-cooled custard. Fold in a quarter of the meringue and then gently fold in the rest. Pour into the prepared ramekins to the very top and smooth evenly. Slide a sharp knife around the rim. Place on the hot baking tray and cook near the top of the oven for 10 minutes.

To Serve:
A little icing sugar

6 Dust with a little sieved icing sugar and serve immediately. If strawberries are not in season, substitute 1 mashed banana, which will work perfectly with the quantities given.

SIMPLE SUMMER PUDDING

Everyone loves Summer Pudding. This version avoids the time spent lining a pudding basin with bread. It is definitely a summer dessert as it would be far too expensive to obtain the right fruits other than during the summer months (May to August), and it wouldn't taste as good.

Utensils Large saucepan and 4 large, bulbous wine glasses

350g/12oz redcurrants
225g/8oz blackcurrants
350g/12oz raspberries
125g/4½oz caster sugar

1 Remove the stalks and mix the berries together with the sugar in a large saucepan, gently heat. As the berries are very delicate, it will only take a few minutes for the heat to penetrate them. When the juices have seeped from the fruit and the sugar has dissolved, they are ready.

8 thin slices of white bread or brioche

2 Remove the crusts from the bread or brioche and cut each slice into small triangles. Place 2 triangles into the bottom of each wine glass and top with a spoonful of the warm berries and juice, which will then soak into the bread.

3 Add a few more triangles of bread to cover the fruit and then spoon in more fruit. Layer it right to the top, finishing with a layer of bread, which you can push gently into the juices. Cover and leave to cool in the fridge.

To Serve:
Additional berries, mint and clotted cream

4 Garnish the pudding with additional berries and mint. Serve with clotted cream.

INDEX

MAIL ORDER INGREDIENTS

Richardson's Smokehouse
– 01394 450103
Simply Sausages
– 020 7394 7776
The Spice Shop
– 020 7221 4448
Peppers by Post
– 01308 897892
The Chocolate Society
– 01423 322230
e-mail: info@chocolate.co.uk
and web site:
www.chocolate.co.uk